Just in case ~

ever shor~

Love Wendy & William ~

D0276812

101 THINGS FOR THE HANDYMAN TO DO

101 THINGS FOR THE HANDYMAN TO DO

A.C. HORTH, F.R.S.A

TEMPUS

Once upon a time, before DIY stores and consumable, disposable household items almost every man was a handyman, having an extensive toolkit designed to repair things around the house for the make-do-and-mend generation. From sharpening the kitchen knives to picture framing, crockery repairs, clock cleaning and making furniture, he was a veritable DIY superman, turning his hand to a multitude of tasks, all designed to make life easier and better for him and his wife.

Many of the topics covered within this volume are as relevant today as they were when it was first published in 1937. Most home handymen will find something new and of interest within the following pages. However, times have changed and in these days of Health and Safety, the Publishers recommend caution while undertaking some of the projects.

First published 1937; This edition 2007

Tempus Publishing Limited
The Mill, Brimscombe Port,
Stroud, Gloucestershire, GL5 2QG
www.tempus-publishing.com

© A.C. Horth, 1937

The right of A.C. Horth to be identified as the Author
of this work has been asserted in accordance with the
Copyrights, Designs and Patents Act 1988.

British Library Cataloguing in Publication Data.
A catalogue record for this book is available from the British Library.

ISBN 978 0 7524 4263 1

Typesetting and origination by Tempus Publishing Limited
Printed in Great Britain by Oaklands Book Service Limited

CONTENTS

CONTENTS

PREFACE

ENCOURAGED by the success of the three previous volumes, and acting on the suggestion that the author should write a book for the handyman in addition to those for Boys, Girls and Little Folks, this new volume in the series of " 101 Things To Do " caters for the man who likes to do the odd jobs about the house and to spend interesting hours in making useful articles of furniture.

The handyman will find in this book information regarding the choice, use and care of tools, instructions for carrying out every-day repairs, not only to household articles, furniture and appliances, but to the fabric of the building, inside and out ; hints on alterations and improvements on painting, polishing and decoration, and on useful processes, and many suggestions for making really useful fitments and pieces of furniture for the home and garden.

It is hoped that the diagrams and photographs will convey most of the necessary information, and for this reason the explanatory text has been kept brief.

A. C. H.

LONDON,
October, 1937.

ACKNOWLEDGMENTS

THE author is indebted to Messrs. Frank Romany Ltd., High Street, Camden Town, N.W.1, for lending and arranging the photographs of tools and for specimen of Hairlok. To Messrs. Samuel Jones & Co., Dryad Handicrafts, Electrical Development Association, Venesta Ltd., Ronuk Ltd., Modern Paints and Finishes Ltd., The Rawlplug Co. Ltd., Singer Manufacturing Co. and Weldons Ltd. for loan of blocks and photographs. To Messrs. Arnold T. Bailey and H. P. Nicholson for permission to use their original prize designs for clock cases, published in *Practical Education*, and to Mr. Frank S. Rolfe for valuable help in photography and the arrangement of the subjects.

THE HOME WORKSHOP

Although there are many jobs round and about the house that the handyman can do with a small equipment of tools, it is a great advantage to have a room set apart for use as a workshop and a place where all the necessary odds and ends can be conveniently stored. A back room or an unused attic, provided the lighting is good, may be converted into an excellent workshop, but failing a room in the house an outside shed should be used.

A minimum size for an outside workshop would be 10 ft. by 8 ft. A window should occupy one of the long sides and should, if possible, face north. The construction of a workshop is not a difficult job, but as sectional buildings ready to bolt together are so low in price, it is often more economical to purchase one than to construct one from the rough timber. In fact, for the handyman who is not greatly skilled in the use of tools, it will be found that the cost of the ready-made shed will be very little more than the cost of the material purchased in the rough at the timber yard.

It is quite unnecessary to begin with a large assortment of tools and appliances. The better way is to begin with a few tools and add to the equipment as the need for it arises. A considerable amount of useful work can be done with comparatively few tools, providing that the necessary equipment is provided.

Many useful appliances can be home-made, but in making tool purchases it is always advisable to buy the best quality from a firm of repute. There are many cheap tools on the market and these, more often than not, give disappointment and do not lead to good work.

Artificial lighting will, no doubt, be required, and as far as possible this should be arranged to give direct rays on to the work bench.

WORK BENCHES

The provision of a work bench is an important consideration. A bench should measure about 5 ft. long and 2 ft. wide, and be made with a stout framework of timber about 3 in. by 3 in., with a front top board, preferably of birch, about 10 in. wide and $1\frac{1}{2}$ in. thick. An ordinary bench screw or a woodworkers metal vice should be fitted. Ready made benches, as shown on page 7, are not expensive, but they should be strong. A light bench may be made more serviceable by securing it to the wall.

When a specially fitted workshop is impracticable, the question of a suitable bench top for use on the kitchen table should be considered. Such a fitment is shown at Fig. 1. The topboard should be of hardwood and measure about 12 in. longer than the table top, and be at least 9 in. wide and $1\frac{1}{4}$ in. thick. At one end screw on a length of hardwood 9 in. by 3 in. and at the other a length of 3 in. by 1 in., as indicated in the sections. On the front screw on a length of board 9 in. wide by 1 in. thick. Bore holes for pegs, as shown, and for a vice use a bench holdfast as indicated. The bench top should be heavy enough to keep in position, but security can be given by G cramps fastened at the back.

A stronger form of bench with a folding top is shown at Fig. 2 and 3 ; the framing is made with deal. The legs are hinged to uprights about 6 in. wide and $1\frac{1}{2}$ in. thick secured to wall plates of 1 in. wood. The legs are framed up as shown and fold back against the wall. With the exception of the left-hand leg, which should be about 2 in. by 2 in., the wood used is 6 in. by $1\frac{1}{2}$ in. The topboard should not be less than $1\frac{1}{4}$ in. thick and stiffened underneath with pieces of the same material. This form of construction will be found quite satisfactory, as it allows for the use of a bench screw.

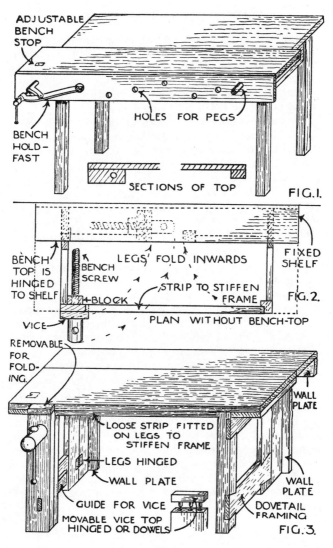

ADJUSTABLE
BENCH
STOP

HOLES FOR PEGS

BENCH
HOLD–
FAST

SECTIONS OF TOP

FIG.1.

BENCH
TOP IS
HINGED
TO SHELF

BENCH
SCREW

LEGS FOLD INWARDS

FIXED
SHELF

STRIP TO STIFFEN
FRAME

FIG.2.

BLOCK

VICE

PLAN WITHOUT BENCH-TOP

REMOVABLE
FOR
FOLD-
ING.

WALL
PLATE

LOOSE STRIP FITTED
ON LEGS TO
STIFFEN FRAME

LEGS HINGED

WALL PLATE

GUIDE FOR VICE

MOVABLE VICE TOP
HINGED OR DOWELS

WALL
PLATE

DOVETAIL
FRAMING

FIG.3.

CUPBOARDS FOR TOOLS

Suitable cupboards or receptacles are essential if tools are to be kept in the best condition. Tool chests can be used, but a cupboard usually is more convenient as the tools are more readily found, it is also an advantage to hang the saws and chisels in positions where the cutting edges are not liable to be damaged.

A suitable cupboard is shown at the top of the next page. The actual dimensions should be determined by the number of tools it is desired to store. It will be seen by the dotted lines that the hand and tenon saws are fitted on one of the doors made large enough for a handsaw about 30 in. long and 6 in. wide, and a tenon saw about 15 in. long and 5 in. wide; the door should, therefore, measure at least 32 in. by 11 in. Allowing for a depth of 5 in. the outside dimensions of the cupboard made of $\frac{3}{4}$ in. wood will be approximately $33\frac{1}{2}$ in. by $23\frac{1}{2}$ in. by 6 in. Partitions and drawers should be arranged at convenient places inside the cupboard, due allowance being made for the projections on the doors, which should be from $1\frac{1}{4}$ in. to $1\frac{1}{2}$ in. The doors should be hinged with strong cross-garnet hinges.

Another form of tool cupboard shown on the bottom of the next page is combined with a sawing stool and is useful when space is limited. The sawing bench should be made with a top of $1\frac{1}{4}$ in. wood about 30 in. long and 6 in. wide to a height of 18 in. or so. The supports should be about 2 in. by 2 in., and the boarding, which is nailed on the ends, 1 in. thick. The doors and bottom boards need not be more than $\frac{3}{4}$ in. thick. Nail together firmly, and attach door with cross garnet hinges. Shelves can be fitted inside if desired. Made to a length of 3 ft. or so with a top board about 9 in. wide and about $1\frac{1}{2}$ in. thick, this type of sawing stool will serve as a bench useful for many purposes.

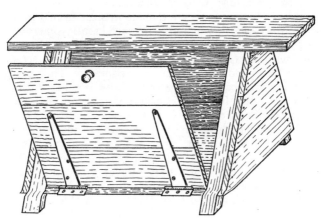

5

TOOLS FOR WOODWORKING

Considerable care should be devoted to the provision of a tool kit. As a rule, only those tools made and sold by firms of repute and experience should be purchased.

The following list contains all the ordinary tools likely to be required by the handyman working in his own workshop.

Handsaw, 24 in. with 8 or 10 teeth to the inch. Tenon Saw, preferably with brass back and a 12 in. blade. Bow Saw, with beech frame and 12 in. blade. Pad Saw, beech handle, heavy ferrule and 10 in. blade. Jack Plane, 14 in. by $2\frac{1}{4}$ in., made of English beech and fitted with double irons. Smoothing Plane, this may be of wood, but preferably of metal with end and side adjustments, lever cap and rosewood fittings. Rebate Plane, known as Rabbit Plane, with skew iron : a 1 in. wide plane is useful, but these planes are made in several widths. Chisels, known as firmer chisels, one each, $\frac{1}{4}$ in., $\frac{3}{8}$ in., $\frac{5}{8}$ in., and 1 in., to begin with ; all with box handles. Mortise Chisels, not essential, may be added as occasion arises. Gouges, Firmer, having the grinding bevel on the outside and, Scribing, with an inside bevel, should be obtained as required ; they are made in sizes from $\frac{1}{4}$ in. to 1 in. Spokeshave, preferably the metal kind ; one round face and one flat face should be provided each 9 in. long with a $1\frac{3}{4}$ in. cutter. Brace and Bit, with set of centre bits and twist bits as required. The Brace should have ball bearing head and ratchet fitting. Hammers, one light Warrington shape and one claw hammer. Screwdrivers, one 8 in. and one fine blade. Mallet, one beech $4\frac{1}{2}$ in. size. Oilstone, one combination carborundum, 6 in. by 2 in. by 1 in., and one slip, $4\frac{1}{2}$ in. long. Oil Can, Marking Gauge, beech. Try Square, all metal 6 in. size. Bevel 8 in., 2 ft. Rule. Mortise Gauge, Pincers, Bradawls and Nail Punch. A Plough Plane should be included if possible.

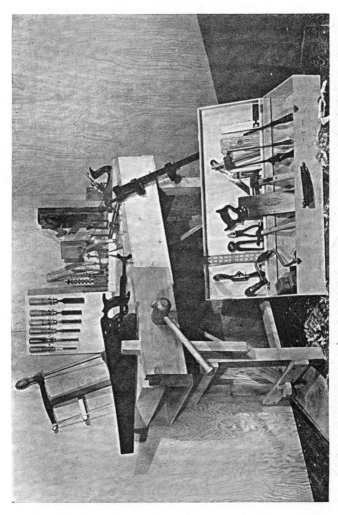

A FOLDING WORK BENCH AND A COLLECTION OF TOOLS FOR WOODWORKING.

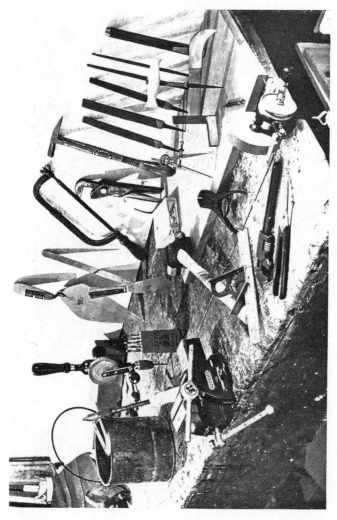

TOOLS FOR METALWORKING AND ODD JOBS.

8

TOOLS FOR METALWORKING AND ODD JOBS

A Hand-drill with double gear, and a 3-jaw chuck to hold drills up to $\frac{1}{4}$ in., as shown in the next page, is an almost indispensable tool. Twist drills of carbon steel, useful for wood and metal, can be obtained as required. The Hacksaw should be adjustable to take blades from 8 in. to 12 in.; blades with 14 to 18 teeth to the inch are required for cutting solid metal, from 22 to 32 for tubing. A 12 in. Steel Rule, a Scriber, Dividers, and Callipers are useful tools to have. Either a Steel Square or one of the more useful combination squares, as shown, should be obtained. Tinman's Snips and Cutting Pliers should be of good quality, cheap qualities of these tools are not satisfactory. An Adjustable Spanner will be needed for tap repairs, and in addition, it is an advantage to have a medium size (either 7 in. or 9 in.) Foot-print gas-pipe wrench.

A Strong Vice similar to that shown in the photograph should be provided and fixed to the bench, but a light clamp-on vice is useful for small work. A Ball Pane Hammer is useful for riveting and an Upholsterer's Hammer will be found useful for a variety of purposes. A few Assorted Files, 6 in. or 8 in., the most useful selection would be two hand files, bastard and smooth cut, two half round, bastard and smooth, with safe edge, two or three warding files, two cabinet rasps, one or two of taper square and round.

The Soldering Bit should be a large one, at least a 1 lb. size is advisable. Other useful tools are a Hand Grinder, a Stock with taps and dies, a Rimer and a Cold Chisel.

A Putty Knife, a Lino Cutting Knife, a Scraper and a Trowel will be useful, as also a Spring Rule and Blow Lamp, these tools should be obtained as they are required.

SHARPENING TOOLS

The sharpening of a cutting tool requires care and knowledge; unless it is carried out properly, successful work is impossible. Odd moments spent in keeping tools ready for service is time well spent.

To begin with the plane iron, remove the cap iron by giving the screw a turn or two and place the bevelled edge on the stone in the position indicated, which shows an angle a little under 30°. Use plenty of oil on the stone and keep the angle constant. When more than $\frac{1}{8}$ in. of sharpening surface has been worn down the iron should be ground to an angle of about 15°. On no account must the flat side of the cutting iron be sharpened. The same method applies to the chisel; in both cases the burr should be removed by stroking the tool on a leather pad.

Saws require setting as well as sharpening, and generally it will be found advisable to get this difficult job carried out by a saw setter. The way in which the alternate teeth are sharpened by the careful use of a three-cornered file is shown on the next page; the even setting of the teeth is also indicated.

The file is used also in sharpening centre bits, twist bits, bradawls and the cutting edge of the marking gauge. In each case a fine file should be used on the surfaces indicated.

Gouges are sharpened with a small piece of oilstone known as a slip, the edges are round, one being a larger radius than the other. The bevel already ground on the tool should be retained, and in the up and down movement of the slip it should be kept to the same angle as the bevel. In this and all other bevelled sharpening edges the flat side of the tool should not be touched with the stone. Any burr caused by sharpening should be removed with a hard leather strop.

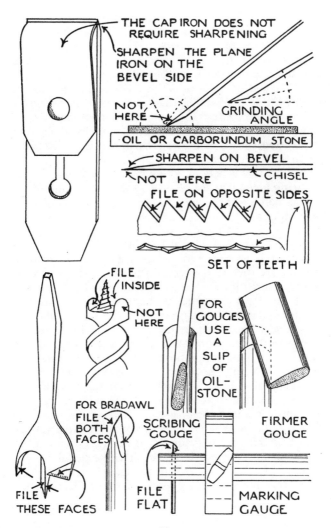

THE CAP IRON DOES NOT REQUIRE SHARPENING

SHARPEN THE PLANE IRON ON THE BEVEL SIDE

NOT HERE

GRINDING ANGLE

OIL OR CARBORUNDUM STONE

SHARPEN ON BEVEL

NOT HERE — CHISEL

FILE ON OPPOSITE SIDES

SET OF TEETH

FILE INSIDE

NOT HERE

FOR GOUGES USE A SLIP OF OIL-STONE

FOR BRADAWL FILE BOTH FACES

SCRIBING GOUGE

FIRMER GOUGE

FILE THESE FACES

FILE FLAT

MARKING GAUGE

11

USING TOOLS

Correct handling in the use of tools is important. In using the handsaw, begin the cut as indicated at Fig. 1 and draw the saw upwards. The best position in sawing is when the eye and hand and saw are in a line. As a rule, the saw cut should be made on the waste side of the line and, as far as possible, the whole length of the saw should be used rather than short cuts using only a portion of the teeth. In using the tenon saw hold it firmly and begin by drawing the blade backwards in the position shown at Fig. 2, remembering to keep the eye directly over the saw.

The bow saw is held in both hands, as shown at Fig. 3, care being taken that the blade is in tension by tightening up the cord; when not in use the cord should be slackened.

The correct method of holding a Jack plane is shown at Fig. 4. It is essential that the sole of the plane should be pressed down firmly to the surface of the wood to be planed. At the beginning of the cut, the downward pressure on the plane is exerted mainly by the left hand, but as forward pressure is applied, the downward pressure is gradually transferred to the right hand. It is essential to good work that the cutting blade should project just enough to take off a thin shaving. If the blade is at all blunt it is impossible to obtain a satisfactory surface. In using the smoothing plane set the cutting iron very finely, hold it firmly in both hands as shown at Fig. 5, and apply pressure evenly throughout the cut. The rebate plane is held as indicated at Fig. 6. The blade should be set with shortest possible projection in order that thin shavings are taken off with each cut.

Chisels must always have the keenest possible edge if they are to do their work properly, and in sharpening on no account should the back of the blade have the

FIG. I.

FIG. 2.

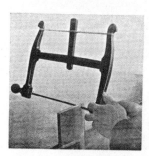

FIG. 3.

FIG. 4.

FIG. 5.

FIG. 6.

FIG. 7.

FIG. 8.

FIG. 9.

FIG. 10.

FIG. 11.

FIG. 12.

slightest bevel. In using a chisel for vertical paring, as shown at Fig. 7, the right hand is used in pressing the chisel downwards, the first finger of the left hand being used as a guide. As a rule a slicing action is more effective than a purely vertical cut. When cutting grooves hold the chisel firmly as shown at Fig. 8. Do not force the chisel unduly through the wood. Aim at thin cuts, and if thin cuts are difficult, sharpen the tool.

The use of the try square and marking knife is important, especially when setting out joints. The best position of the hands when using these tools is shown at Fig. 9. Do not use the cut line when marking out chamfers. As a rule the scribing tools—knife and gauge—should be used when indicating the position of saw and chisel cuts. Preliminary lines can be made with a pencil when marking out, but in all cases make a cut line for groove, tenon and mortise cuts.

The spokeshave is an exceedingly useful tool, it is held quite lightly between the fingers as shown at Fig. 10, and should not be grasped in the hands. It is a tool to be used with care and always the blade must be quite keen.

Although separate notes are given on page 10 relative to methods of tool sharpening, an illustration is given at Fig. 11 showing the method of removing the cutting iron of the plane. A light tap with the mallet is generally sufficient, for the wedge which keeps the blade in position should not be driven in tightly. The mallet should be used very lightly when the wedge is inserted; and it should not be used to adjust the blade itself, this should be done with a hammer.

The correct method of holding a chisel when sharpening is shown at Fig. 12. It is most important to keep the angle constant during the operation; the method of handling the plane iron is similar. The bevel side shown is the only part to be sharpened.

PLANING HINTS

Unless wood is used for outdoor carpentry and building operations, it is usual to plane it smooth and true. As a rule it is not difficult to plane smooth, but as all wood is liable to warp and twist during the process of seasoning, it becomes necessary to true up the surfaces in addition to getting them quite smooth. True surfaces are essential, particularly in making joints.

Timber can be obtained machined-planed to size, but generally the finish is not sufficiently good for the best work, also it is even then liable to warp a little. The test for a warped board is shown at Fig. 1, and consists of placing two straight edges across the board and bringing the eye in line with the top edges of the strips. Any divergence from the level can be seen at once, because one strip will be higher at one end than the other as at Fig. 2. The opposite corners of the board may show a twist as shown at Fig. 3, in which the true level is represented by dotted lines. To remedy such a fault the wood must be planed down to the level of the lower parts indicated by the arrow head.

Having levelled the main surface of the wood, one edge should be planed and trued as shown at Figs. 4 and 5, but it is necessary to make quite sure that the length is true and it should be tested with a straight edge as at Fig. 6. When true, mark the wood as shown at Fig. 7. The width and thickness of the wood should always be gauged from the face marks as shown.

In glueing two boards together as shown at Fig. 8, the touching surfaces must be quite true, and immediately after glueing move backwards and forwards, in the direction of the arrows, to exclude all possible glue. Although a glued joint may be left undisturbed until set, it is advisable to use a cramp as shown at Fig. 5 on page 19.

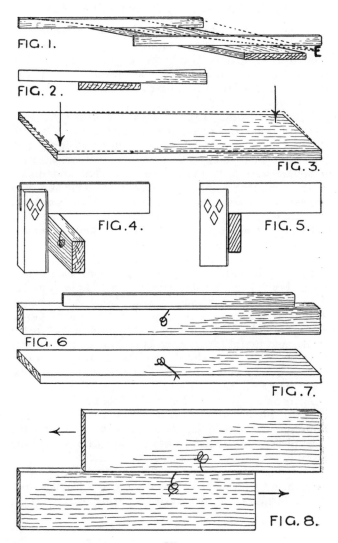

FIG. I.

FIG. 2.

FIG. 3.

FIG. 4.

FIG. 5.

FIG. 6

FIG. 7.

FIG. 8.

17

APPLIANCES FOR WOODWORK

Sawing Board. Fig. 1. For use with a tenon saw, this board is made from 10 in. to 12 in. long and from 5 in. to 6 in. wide. The blocks on the end should be from 1½ in. to 2 in. wide and 1 in. thick. They can be the full width of the board or leave a space of 1 in. or so on the right-hand side.

Shooting Board. Fig. 2. Used for planing the long edges of thin strips or trueing up right angle ends ; the the top board should be about 18 in. or so long, 4 in. wide and 1 in. thick with a strip of hardwood 1 in., in square section, let in near the end. The underboard of the same length should be about 7 in. wide and need not be more than ½ in. or ¾ in. thick. Two battens of 2 in. by 1 in. wood serve to stiffen the board at the ends.

Cramp. Fig. 3. This can be made to any convenient length from wood machine-planed to 2 in. by 1 in. thick. The cross pieces should be about 12 in. long, one is fixed securely with screws, the other is provided with a round beech peg 1 in. diameter, fitting in holes bored at intervals along the long length. Long and narrow wedges as at Fig. 4 should be provided for use as shown at Fig. 5. Another form of cramp used with twisted string, and useful for framing, is shown at Fig. 6. Four of these corner pieces should be prepared from hardwood such as beech, with a section of about 2 in. by 1 in ; the projecting arms can be from 2 in. to 6 in. long.

Mitre Sawing Block. Fig. 7. This should be made of beech or birch with the wood at least 1 in. thick. The bottom piece should be about 12 in. by 5 in. and the side pieces 3 in. wide. Considerable care should be taken in setting out and sawing the mitre cuts.

Straightedges. A pair of straightedges about 18 in. by 2 in. by ¼ in. planed up quite true and parallel from beech or mahogany are needed for testing.

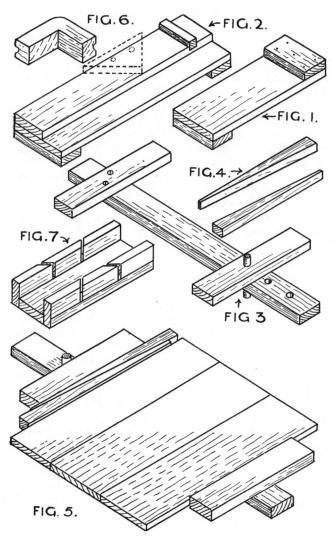

FIG. 6.

←FIG. 2.

←FIG. 1.

FIG. 4.→

FIG. 7→

FIG 3

FIG. 5.

COMMON JOINTS

There are only a few joints that are commonly used in constructional work. The corner halving shown at Fig. 1 is quite simple, as also the same joint used as shown at Fig. 2. With ordinary care in marking out and cutting on the waste side of the line, no difficulty should be experienced in making a good joint.

The mortise and tenon joint is shown on a corner at Fig. 3, and on the side at Fig. 4; another form, known as the haunched mortise and tenon is at Fig. 5. Care must be taken in marking out to ensure that the thickness of the tenon equals the width of the mortise. The mortise gauge is useful for this joint. As a rule it is advisable to set the mortise gauge to correspond with the width of the chisel used in cutting the mortise. In setting out the haunched mortise and tenon it is advisable to leave a projection on the mortise end and cut it off after the joint is made. The mortise and tenon joint can be strengthened with wedges, in this case the sides of the mortise should be enlarged to take up the space occupied by the wedges.

The dovetail halving joint at Fig. 6 is particularly useful. The dovetail can be carried right through or stopped as shown at Fig. 7. In making the joint, shown open at Figs. 8 and 9, the latter portion should be made first and fitted in position so that the exact shape of the dovetail can be marked. The common dovetail joint shown closed at Fig. 10 and open at Fig. 11 is the strongest form of corner joint and much used in cabinet-work. The pins should be set out and cut before the sockets are marked out; actually there is little difference between the lapped dovetail and the common dovetail. Another form of the joint, used commonly for drawer construction is shown at Fig. 12. Apart from the extra care required it is made similarly to the joint at Fig. 10.

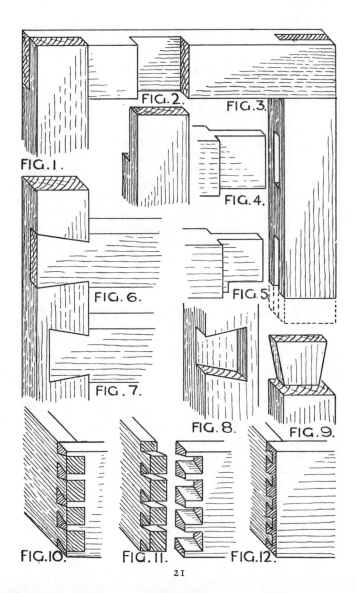

FIG. 1.

FIG. 2.

FIG. 3.

FIG. 4.

FIG. 5.

FIG. 6.

FIG. 7.

FIG. 8.

FIG. 9.

FIG. 10.

FIG. 11.

FIG. 12.

PASSE-PARTOUT BINDING

As a means of framing pictures rapidly, the use of prepared binding is most effective. The method is simple and economical and with the large range of colours available in the binding material, pictures can be framed attractively and durably.

Pictures can be framed up close without margin, may be mounted on plain or tinted cardboard or provided with a cut-out mount. First decide on the actual size the picture is to be and then cut a piece of glass to the same dimensions. Provide also to the same size a piece of cardboard or strawboard for the back.

There are several methods of hanging passe-partout frames, the most suitable are those having small brass rings attached to narrow strips of metal, similar to paper fasteners, or short loops of tape. Two slits have to be made in the back so that the loops can be passed through and secured to the back.

Cut the binding into lengths about $\frac{1}{2}$ in. longer than the sides of the glass, moisten one long strip about half the width with a damp sponge or soft brush, place the top of the glass and back complete on the strip while it is still thoroughly wet. Press down firmly and rub evenly. In order to make sure that the edge of the binding is parallel with the glass, it is a good plan to rule out a guide on a piece of paper and place underneath.

The same method is followed for the other long side, taking care that the strip is parallel. The remaining half of the binding is moistened and folded over on the back. Trim the corners to a mitre, cut off the ends to leave about $\frac{1}{8}$ in. to fold in and finally bind up the short sides and trim off close.

Deep binding can be done by covering narrow strips of cardboard with strips of binding and securing the strips to the previously bound glass, care in mitreing the corners is essential.

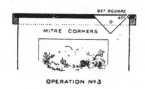

By courtesy of Samuel Jones & Co.

A PASTEL SKETCH MOUNTED ON STRAWBOARD
WITH CUT-OUT MOUNT.

24

MOUNTING PICTURES

A mount is generally used in preparing either a water colour, a pastel or an etching for framing. Mounting boards are obtainable in various thicknesses and are made in standard measurements, as 30 in. by 22 in. and 21 in. by 19 in., approximating to Imperial and Royal sizes. The thicknesses are 2, 4 and 6 sheet, the latter being approximately a little under $\frac{1}{8}$ in. thick.

In preparing the picture it is mounted first of all on a piece of cardboard of a suitable size to provide a pleasing margin. Use clean paste and place under pressure until dry. Border lines are drawn on the outside of the picture to indicate the position of the opening of the top mount ; care should be taken that the lines are parallel with the edges of the mount.

The selected mounting board is now placed under the picture and a pin driven into the mount through each corner of the pencilled border. With the pin holes as corners, draw frame lines with very faint pencil lines. The difficult part of the work is to cut out the middle of the mount with a sloping cut. Mount cutting knives are obtainable, but a pocket knife with a thin, sharp blade can be used. If the mount is small, it will be possible to cut a short straight line without difficulty, but with a long line it is advisable to use a ruler, preferably a steel one.

It is not always necessary to use white mounts, they may be obtained tinted or in various colours. For some pictures, a pleasing effect can be obtained by using grey or brown mounts. The bevelled edges of the cut out portion may be left white or they may be gilded. It will be seen on page 29 that the mounts have what is known as a washed border, they are not inexpensive and can be obtained in any size.

PICTURE FRAME MAKING

The method of measuring up for framing is shown at Fig. 1. First of all it is necessary to know the sight sizes, that is the area of the picture, including the mount if used, to be shown inside the frame. The rebate sizes indicate the outside dimensions of the picture or mount, the size of the glass and the backing board. The overall sizes are those of the outside of the frame.

The corners of wooden frames are mitred as indicated at Fig. 2, and the method of marking out the length of moulding is shown at Fig. 3. In the latter diagram, the measurements given are those of the rebate sizes and this is the safest method of marking out the pieces. It will be understood that a large number of different mouldings are available and, unless the rebate size is taken, there is likely to be difficulty in making an accurate frame.

The mitres should be very accurately cut with a saw on a perfectly true mitre block; one form is shown on page 19. The particular block shown at Fig. 6 is made of hardwood, generally beech, and in order to ensure accuracy the top portion should be about 3 in. or more wide.

In nailing the mitres, fix one of the sides in the vice and allow the other portion to project a little as shown at Fig. 4. When the nailing is being done the upper portion will slide down to form a clean joint. This applies to all mitres nailed up without a corner cramp and can be done with any of the mouldings shown in section at Fig. 5.

Two methods of strengthening the corners of heavy moulding are shown at Figs. 7 and 8. In the former, a thin strip is glued into a saw cut and afterwards sawn off and trimmed smooth, and in the latter an angle plate is screwed on at the back. When using either of the methods above, it is advisable to cramp up the frame during the process.

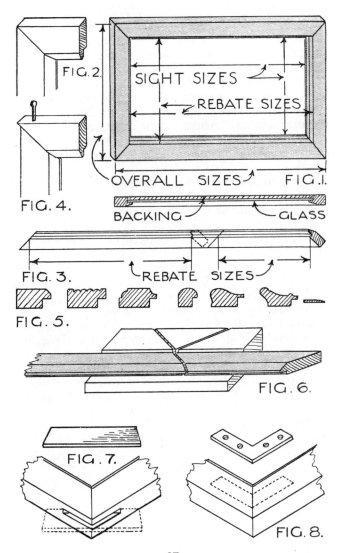

FIG. 2.

SIGHT SIZES

REBATE SIZES

OVERALL SIZES

FIG. 4.

FIG. 1.

BACKING

GLASS

FIG. 3.

REBATE SIZES

FIG. 5.

FIG. 6.

FIG. 7.

FIG. 8.

27

FRAMING PICTURES

The choice of a suitable frame for a picture requires consideration. Tradition has given the oil painting a heavy gilt frame, the water-colour a thin gold frame, and the engraving an oak moulding, but modern taste has made considerable alterations. The next two pages give some indication as to suitable frames for water-colours, pastels, etchings and photographs. Fairly substantial and decorative frames are still used for oil paintings, but individual taste enters very considerably in this case.

The pastel at the bottom of the page (Fig. 3) is framed in limed oak with a mount with a washed border. The water-colour at Fig. 1 has a gold frame and a deep cut mount with a washed border. The pastel in the centre of the page (Fig. 2) has a plain bevelled moulding, silvered, with a plain white mount. The latter frame, made of oak, previously held an engraving, but it was scraped, sized and painted with silver paint, although aluminium paint is quite suitable.

Etchings are usually framed up as shown on page 30. The example at the top of the page on the left indicates a method of dealing with a small etching with a comparatively large cut-out mount. The moulding is in black enamel with a half-round edge. The large etching at the bottom of the page is framed in black flat moulding and the picture is mounted with a cut-out white mount. Engravings can be treated effectively in this way.

Photographs, especially portraits, can be treated similarly to etchings, although a cut-out mount is not always necessary. It is usually more pleasing to have a wider margin at the bottom. In all cases it is advisable to cover the back of the frame with paper to prevent dust entering at the rebates.

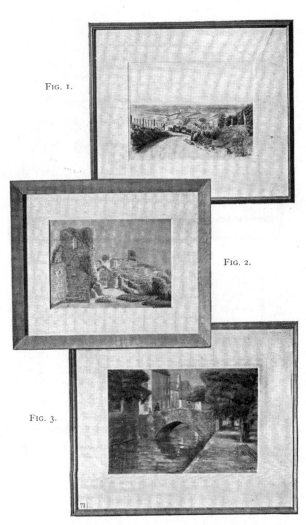

Fig. 1.

Fig. 2.

Fig. 3.

FRAMING PASTELS AND WATER-COLOURS.

29

FRAMED ETCHINGS AND A FRAMED PHOTOGRAPHIC
PORTRAIT.

GILDING

Gilding can be done with gold leaf or gold paint, the former is preferable although more expensive. Gold paint is available in powder form or mixed with a medium. Gold leaf is obtained in small books containing approximately 25 leaves measuring about 3 ins. square; it is used in conjunction with gold size.

In regilding a frame or other article, clean thoroughly with lukewarm water containing a little soda. Use a fairly stiff brush to get into the crevices and rinse with clean water. Fill up all cracks with putty or plastic wood, and in the event of damaged mouldings, the latter material can be used as it can be carved quite easily when hard. To apply gold leaf, first wet a portion of the frame with size and leave until tacky, pick off a leaf of gold with a clean dry knife without touching it with the fingers, place it in position and blow on it to force it into contact with the surface. The leaf is now pressed down into contact with the surface with a pad of cotton wool and finally burnished with an agate or bone burnisher.

To apply gold paint, clean up the frame in the same way as above, mix the paint thoroughly and apply evenly with a camel hair brush. Cheap gold paint is never satisfactory, use the best quality as it does not tarnish so rapidly. Transparent shellac varnish or cellulose will often brighten up a gold painted frame.

In dealing with new gilded work, the surface should be made quite smooth and free from blemishes. The surface should be coated with size or a good undercoat of white paint applied, When dry the surface should be coated with gold size and left until tacky, and it is advisable, especially when dealing with large surfaces, to gild small portions at a time. When using gold leaf always work on a large sheet of paper so that unused scraps of leaf can be collected.

SHARPENING SCISSORS AND KNIVES

The cutting edges of scissors can be kept in perfect condition if they are sharpened from time to time, and to do this effectively use a good sharpening stone with a flat surface. One of the most useful forms of hone for household use is the carborundum stone, provided with a fine surface on one side and a coarse surface on the other. The stone should be mounted in a recess on a wooden block to prevent breakage.

It will be seen that the meeting edges of the scissor blades are bevelled to the angle shown at Fig. 1 ; in sharpening it is essential to keep to this bevel, the correct position being shown at Fig. 2. Use plenty of oil and press firmly on the stone while each blade in turn is rubbed backwards and forwards. On no account should the flat surfaces of the blades be placed on the stone.

After sharpening, examine the scissors as at Fig. 3 to see that the tips of the blades touch at the top ; if they are loose, tighten up the screw. If the screw has worn loose, it can be tightened by a few taps with a hammer and thus formed into a rivet.

Pocket knives and similar cutting edges are sharpened in the way shown at Fig. 4. In this case there should be no bevel, but each side of the blade should be evenly tapered as at Fig. 5.

Keep the blade flat on the stone, press it down firmly backwards and forwards to produce a keen edge. The effect of tilting the blade is to form a bevel as at Fig. 6 ; particular care should be taken to prevent this. The blade should be stropped after sharpening on the stone, using a strip of leather, preferably glued on a block of wood, to remove the wire edge. When not in use, the stone should be kept in a covered box to prevent dust filling the pores, and clean with paraffin from time to time to keep in condition.

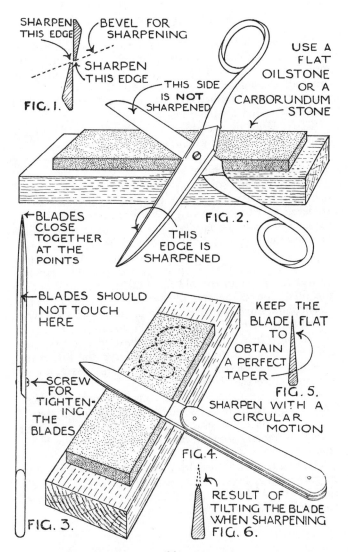

SHARPEN THIS EDGE — BEVEL FOR SHARPENING

SHARPEN THIS EDGE

FIG. 1.

THIS SIDE IS **NOT** SHARPENED

USE A FLAT OILSTONE OR A CARBORUNDUM STONE

FIG. 2.

THIS EDGE IS SHARPENED

BLADES CLOSE TOGETHER AT THE POINTS

BLADES SHOULD NOT TOUCH HERE

SCREW FOR TIGHTENING THE BLADES

FIG. 3.

KEEP THE BLADE FLAT TO OBTAIN A PERFECT TAPER

FIG. 5.

SHARPEN WITH A CIRCULAR MOTION

FIG. 4.

RESULT OF TILTING THE BLADE WHEN SHARPENING FIG. 6.

SOFT SOLDERING

Failure in the use of the soldering bit is due mainly to the lack of care in cleaning up the work and in the use of a bit too small to retain the heat long enough to melt all the solder. It is essential that both the soldering bit and the surface to be coated with solder should be of the same temperature.

Use a large bit weighing at least 1 lb., made with a long piece of copper as shown on the next page. Provide an old file with the end sharpened for use as a scraper, and some emery cloth.

To prepare for soldering, first remove every scrap of dirt and grease, then scrape thoroughly the part to be soldered to expose the bright surface of the metal. As soon as the surface is clean, cover it over with a film of paste flux to prevent the air getting to it.

Heat up the bit, not red hot, but hot enough to heat a stick of solder placed on it. Now quickly clean the end of the bit with the old file and dip it in and out of the flux. Place the end of the stick of solder on the cleaned and fluxed portion of the bit and it will run over it and form a tinned surface as indicated on the diagram.

The bit is held on the portion to be soldered and when sufficient heat has been transferred from the bit to the article to be soldered, the solder will run. Extra solder is applied direct as shown.

It will be seen that the soldering bit must be in itself hot enough to melt the solder placed against it, but it must be sufficiently hotter than the melting point of solder to transfer some of its heat without cooling it too much.

Given a really hot bit with a properly tinned end, clean bright surfaces covered with flux (if possible, previously tinned) there should be no difficulty in carrying out successful soldering.

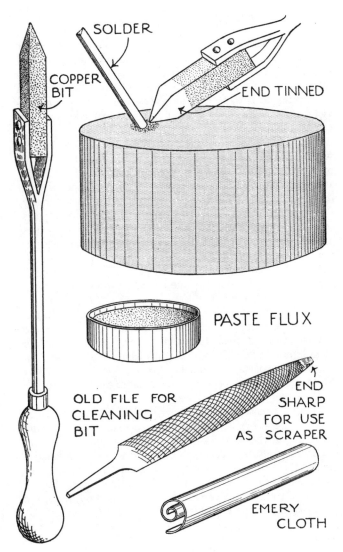

SOLDER

COPPER BIT

END TINNED

PASTE FLUX

OLD FILE FOR CLEANING BIT

END SHARP FOR USE AS SCRAPER

EMERY CLOTH

CROCKERY REPAIRS

It is not always possible to repair broken crockery or earthenware, but there are many kitchen utensils such as the casserole shown at Fig. 1 that may be repaired satisfactorily. As a rule it is not worth the trouble involved in joining up broken dinner plates, but when the breakage is on the edge, as shown at Fig. 3, an effective join can be made.

With china and decorative pottery it is generally worth while to repair breakages. The important thing to remember is to carry out the work as soon as possible after the damage has occurred. The presence of dust on the fracture makes it difficult to join the parts closely.

There are many kinds of cement available for repairs, their use depends on the particular form of material used in the manufacture. In the case of casseroles and similar pots made of comparatively coarse clay, a useful form of cement is that known as " Stixit." It is available in tube form, and is easily applied. Such glues as Seccotine or Croid are also useful.

The first essential is cleanliness, the parts to be joined must be perfectly clean, free from dust and grease. It is also essential that the parts to be joined should be completely covered with a thin film of adhesive, the thinner the coating the better. In applying the adhesive avoid air bubbles, they are a frequent cause of trouble and prevent a perfectly close joint.

Finally, pressure must be applied in the right place ; in many positions there may be great difficulty in using pressure at the correct point. A suitable method of cramping is shown at Figs. 2, 3 and 4, using whipcord rather than ordinary string. Gummed paper strip, of great value in effecting repairs, is also shown at Fig. 4. When all the surplus cement has been expelled, it should be allowed to harden and then scraped off.

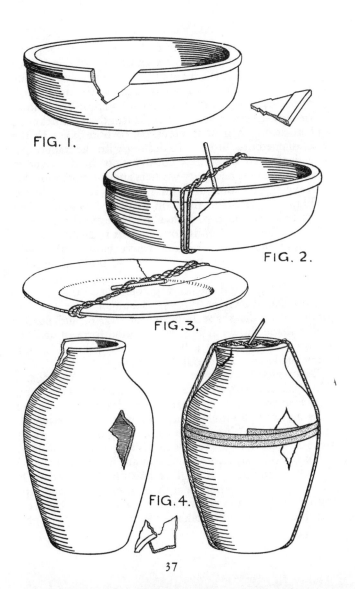

FIG. 1.

FIG. 2.

FIG.3.

FIG. 4.

37

RIVETING

Rivets enter so much into constructional work in wood as well as in metal, that a knowledge of the various forms of rivets and the manner of their fastening is quite necessary. For use with wood framing, the usual form of rivet is shown at Fig. 1, its most common application is for deck-chairs. Rivets vary in length and thickness, and in fitting them it is necessary to bore holes to the exact diameter required. In dealing with the framework of a deck-chair or similar construction, fit the rivet in position with the necessary washers and cut off the surplus to leave a projection of from $\frac{1}{8}$ in. to $\frac{1}{4}$ in. as indicated at Fig. 2. Place the rivet on a metal block and then hammer over the top with a fairly heavy hammer as shown at Fig. 3. Continuous strokes with the hammer are more effective than a few heavy blows ; the main purpose of the hammering is to spread the metal gradually.

In riveting metal sheets together, place the rivet in position as shown at Fig. 4. Hammer over the top gradually to the shape indicated at Fig. 6, and finally, to the shape shown at Fig. 7. A good form of anvil is shown at Fig. 5, it is a flat iron mounted in a strong frame made of wood about 1 in. thick.

Bi-furcated rivets are useful for many purposes. Although not so strong as the ordinary kind of rivet, they are very handy, especially when dealing with leather belts and for all similar purposes where great strength is not needed. With care in hammering over the prongs there is usually no difficulty in making a neat fastening.

To remove old rivets, as shown at Fig. 10, first file off the top as indicated at Fig. 11 and place the underside of the plate on a short length of tubing. A few taps with a nail punch as shown at Fig. 12 will drive the rivet out, but care should be taken to keep the punch upright.

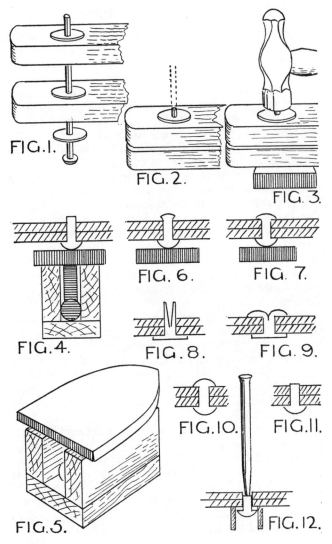

FIG. 1.

FIG. 2.

FIG. 3.

FIG. 4.

FIG. 6.

FIG. 7.

FIG. 5.

FIG. 8.

FIG. 9.

FIG. 10.

FIG. 11.

FIG. 12.

CHAIR AND TABLE REPAIRS

Frequent trouble in chairs is caused by excessive strain or by the shrinkage of the joints connecting the seat rails with the legs. In the case of a loose joint, the frame should be cramped up and either metal or wood brackets screwed on as at Fig. 1. A neater method of repair, shown at Fig. 2, consists in fitting leg braces made of pressed steel as shown at Fig. 3; these braces can be obtained for use with square or round legs. Fig. 2 shows also two ways of fitting small hard wood brackets suitable when leg braces are not available.

Although a well-made deck-chair will last many years without repair, the joints are liable to shrink, especially if the framework has been exposed to the weather. The diagrams at Figs. 4 and 5 illustrate some of the weak points. When the joints work loose at the positions marked P, they should be strengthened by driving a wire nail or panel pin in the direction indicated. In cases where the tenon does not go through the wood, a screw can be driven into the end as shown in the separate illustration.

Rivets at the points marked R may be renewed quite easily by following the directions given on page 38. New canvas covering should be secured by means of clout rails, ordinary tin tacks are not advisable. All the old nails should be pulled out when the worn canvas is stripped off. When attaching the new canvas, always make a double fold before nailing, as shown in the separate detail.

Table joints can be strengthened by using steel brackets as shown at Fig. 6. Care should be taken to enlarge the angle of the bracket to allow for the slope on the inside of the leg. Slender table legs and also chair legs which have been fractured as indicated at Fig. 7, can be repaired by the insertion of a birch dowel. Great care must be taken in using the twist bit when boring to ensure that the holes are opposite each other.

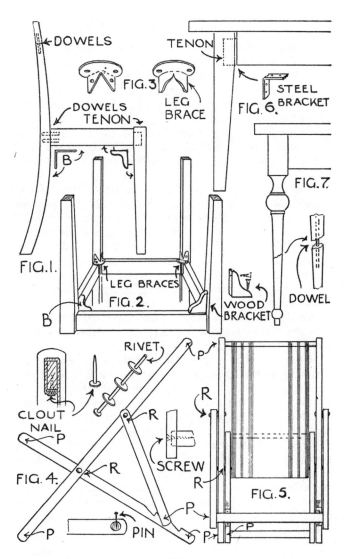

←DOWELS

FIG. 3.

LEG BRACE

DOWELS
TENON

B

FIG. 1.

LEG BRACES

FIG. 2.

B

TENON

STEEL BRACKET
FIG. 6.

FIG. 7.

WOOD BRACKET

DOWEL

RIVET

P

CLOUT NAIL

P

R

SCREW

R

FIG. 4.

R

P

PIN

P

P

R

R

P

FIG. 5.

P

P

41

SIMPLE UPHOLSTERY

Owing to the introduction of new materials much of the difficulty of upholstery has disappeared. In dealing with a pin-cushion seat, that particular form of seating carried out without springs, all that is necessary is to strip the old seating and carefully withdraw the nails. If the webbing is old and has given way in places, it can be renewed in the manner shown at the bottom of the next page. It is essential that the webbing should be of the best quality and well stretched when it is being secured.

But with the use of Hairlok, a new form of hair seating obtainable in several thicknesses, it is possible to do without webbing and instead a piece of plywood may be secured to the frame. Hairlok is made of pure hair teased or lightly worked into a mould. This springy mass is coated with latex rubber and is then vulcanised. It is perfectly hygienic, does not lose its elasticity and can be washed if necessary. It can be cut with scissors to the shape required. In using the material, it is placed between two layers of hessian and covered with cretonne tapestry or whatever form of covering is required.

If the chair has a spring seat, there is no need to use webbing on the frame, just a covering of plywood to fill up the seat space. A spring unit of the required size is now placed on the board, secured with staples and covered with hessian lightly tacked to the frame. A layer of Hairlok is placed on top of the spring unit and covered with hessian prior to the fitting of the seat covering. With the exercise of a little care any form of seat can be upholstered in this way. Spring units suitable for arm chairs are available and are just as easily fitted in position. Careful measurements should be made when ordering the spring units ; as a rule they should fit neatly on the framing.

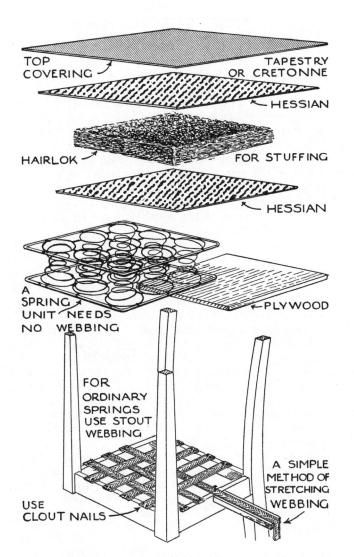

TOP COVERING

TAPESTRY OR CRETONNE

HESSIAN

HAIRLOK

FOR STUFFING

HESSIAN

A SPRING UNIT NEEDS NO WEBBING

PLYWOOD

FOR ORDINARY SPRINGS USE STOUT WEBBING

A SIMPLE METHOD OF STRETCHING WEBBING

USE CLOUT NAILS

43

RESEATING IN CANE

Six stages in recaning are shown opposite. First remove the old cane, and punch out the holes from underneath. Wash the framework with warm water and a hard brush. Begin by inserting a length of No. 2 cane in the centre hole at the back. Wedge it firmly with a peg, bring the cane to the correct hole in the front and peg it down. The cane is brought up through the next hole in front and carried to the correct hole at the back and pegged down. Continue on both sides until the whole of the seat is covered with parallel rows. With seats narrower at the back, place the cane in appropriate holes. When a join is needed bring the end up through the next hole and leave it projecting. Begin a new cane in the same way.

In stage two, the same process is followed, but the canes are across and on the top of the first lot. The third stage is a repetition of the first stage with the canes on top of the second layer. Actual weaving begins with the fourth stage, in which the cane is carried from side to side, each strand in turn being threaded over the canes of the third stage and under those of the first stage.

In the fifth stage No. 3 cane is used and it is threaded diagonally over two and under two. The sixth stage consists of diagonal threading over three and under three. Finish by driving small pegs in every alternate hole to secure the cane and prevent sagging.

To complete the caning, provide four lengths of beading cane and some fine cane for securing it in position.

Insert one end of a length of beading cane at a corner, bring it over to the next corner. Secure the length by threading the fine cane through the holes left unpegged, loop it over the beading cane and continue on all sides. Finish with a peg at the four corners to keep the beading in position.

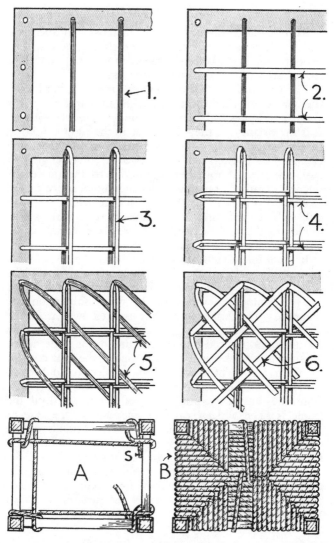

45

RUSH SEATING

Rush seating is not difficult, the material is inexpensive, and for those who live in country districts, there will be no difficulty in gathering a sufficient supply. The best rushes are those which grow near the sea.

The rushes should be dried after gathering, but before they are used, they must be soaked in warm water for about 15 minutes and then placed under a cloth to mellow. It is important that they should be in the right condition before being used, if not sufficiently moist they will crack when twisted. Usually two or three lengths of rush are twisted together, according to the degree of fineness required, but much depends on the size of the rushes. It may happen that the thicker half of one rush will twist to the same diameter as two thinner rushes. Some practice will be needed before the material can be twisted to a uniform thickness.

It is advisable to begin with a stool and at A on page 45 is shown the method of beginning the wrapping. Start by securing the twisted rush as indicated at S and carry it round the frame in the order shown on the diagram. The rushes should be twisted away from the worker and when adding new strands, knot the new strand round the old one so that the join is underneath. As soon as a pocket is formed at each of the four corners by the crossing of the rush, short pieces and broken rushes should be packed in the space from underneath. Continue with the same order of wrapping until the frame is filled at least on one side, and in the case of oblong frames, as at B the final set of strands at the centre will have to be worked from back to front in the form of a figure eight until the seat is filled.

It is a good plan to pull an old rush seat apart and note carefully how the strands are wrapped and tied. The illustration at the bottom of the next page shows a typical seating.

A MODERN APPLICATION OF CANE SEATING.

RUSH SEATED CHAIR AND STOOL.
Photographs by Dryad Handicrafts.

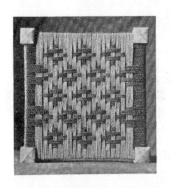 

Photographs by Dryad Handicrafts.

48

SEA GRASS SEATING

Seagrass is a modern product and is rapidly taking the place of twisted rush. It is much easier to use, it does not require to be kept moist during working, and, being obtainable in long lengths, much trouble and time is saved by frequent joins.

It is advisable to wind the seagrass on a shuttle cut from a piece of stiff cardboard, measuring about 8 in. by 3 in., with a V cut at each end ; this will take about 10 yards, a convenient length to use.

The method of weaving is similar to that of rush, described on page 46, but it is possible by the use of various colours to form very interesting patterns. The photographs shown on the opposite page give an indication of the possibilities of the material. It is obtainable in two thicknesses, fine and medium in natural colour, or in orange, scarlet, royal blue, emerald and brown. As the material is difficult to dye, being dark in colour, there is a tendency for the colour to vary slightly with successive dyeings. It is, therefore, advisable to secure sufficient material for the work in hand. Approximately $1\frac{1}{2}$ lbs. of medium seagrass is required for a stool or seat about 12 in. square.

Another useful material is seating cord, now obtainable in similar colouring to seagrass ; it makes very attractive seats and is easily worked. It is made in fine 3-ply, 2-ply and single ply, the latter requires 1 lb. to seat a stool 12 in. by 12 in.

It will be seen in the photographs that the strands of seagrass or cord are interwoven in groups of three or more strands. Patterns are evolved by having separate colour groups, and by using two or more colours in each group. Joins in seagrass or cord should be made with a reef knot and so arranged that they are underneath. Sea grass is equally suitable for chairs and may be used to replace a cane seat.

CLOCK CLEANING

The stoppage of a clock or its failure to keep good time can be traced usually to an accumulation of dust or to the pivots having become clogged with oil. Breakage of the main or hairspring is an infrequent happening ; renewal in this case should be carried out by an expert. Before any attempt is made to clean the movement, the arrangement of the train of wheels and how they are fitted in position should be understood.

A typical movement is shown in front view at Fig. 1 and in plan at Fig. 2. A represents the mainspring, B one of the plates of the frame, C is the main wheel, D is the clickwheel on the main wheel, E is the lantern pinion on the second wheel F, G is the minute wheel and H gives the position of the minute wheel pinion. J is the lantern pinion of the third wheel K, L is the lantern pinion of the escape wheel M, N is the pinion of the motion work wheel O. The crutch which engages with the escape wheel is at P, the lower end of the crutch, shown in the side view, engages with the pendulum rod.

The mechanism of a simple alarm clock is shown in the lower portion of the next page.

Before attempting any extensive cleaning, the train of wheels should be examined, and in places where dust has accumulated it should be wiped off with a small camel-hair brush, and another brush used in applying a minute quantity of oil, purest machine or 3 in 1 oil should be used. If it is found that the pivot holes are clogged with oil, dip a brush in some petrol and clean them before applying fresh oil. With a clock long neglected the whole of the mechanism should be dipped in a bath of petrol, then cleaned with a soft brush, finally apply oil to all the running parts.

In the event of damaged wheels or other mechanical defects, it will be advisable to obtain expert assistance.

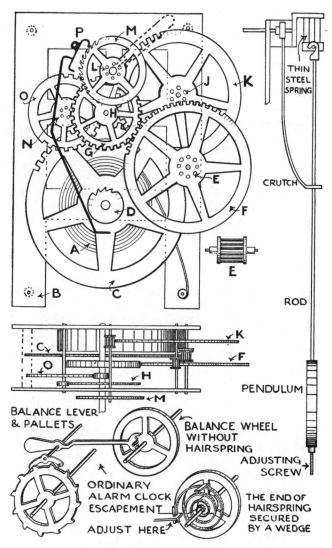

THIN STEEL SPRING

CRUTCH

ROD

E

PENDULUM

ADJUSTING SCREW

BALANCE LEVER & PALLETS

BALANCE WHEEL WITHOUT HAIRSPRING

ORDINARY ALARM CLOCK ESCAPEMENT

ADJUST HERE

THE END OF HAIRSPRING SECURED BY A WEDGE

CLOCK CASES

Excellent clock movements are often contained in old-fashioned marble cases not in keeping with modern decoration. The photographs opposite illustrate the attractive possibilities of a wooden case within the capabilities of the average home craftsman.

The design at the top, by Arnold T. Bailey, is an excellent example of the use of oak and walnut. It is pleasing in shape and decoration, and of sufficient weight and stability to prevent it being easily moved.

A new clock face and frame can be obtained to suit an old movement, or a new movement purchased to conform with the proportion and size of the case. Suitable measurements for the case would be an overall length of 10 in. and a height of $6\frac{3}{4}$ in. The case containing the movements should be in $\frac{3}{8}$ in. oak, measuring $6\frac{1}{2}$ in. wide and $5\frac{3}{4}$ in. high, with a depth of $2\frac{1}{4}$ in. The supports on the sides should be of walnut, 5 in. high, 2 in. wide at the bottom, $1\frac{3}{4}$ in. at the top, and tapered from $\frac{7}{8}$ in. into $\frac{5}{8}$ in. The outside of the supports are buttresses of oak strips, $4\frac{1}{2}$ in. by $1\frac{1}{2}$ in. tapering to $1\frac{1}{4}$ in. and $\frac{5}{8}$ in. to $\frac{7}{16}$ in. The base is rectangular, 10 in. by $2\frac{3}{8}$ in. by 1 in. The top joints should be mitred, bottom joints butted and base and buttresses screwed and glued.

The case designed by H. P. Nicholson is made in oak decorated with gouge cuts and finished by fuming and wax polish. The outside dimensions are 10 in. by $7\frac{3}{4}$ in. by $3\frac{3}{4}$ in. The sides of the case are $6\frac{3}{4}$ in. by 3 in. by $\frac{5}{8}$ in., the top and the bottom are the same width and thickness and $9\frac{1}{4}$ in. long, the corners being dovetailed together.

The front and back are $\frac{5}{8}$ in. thick and are tongued into grooves cut on the inside of the frame. The front is recessed $\frac{1}{2}$ in. to allow for the inside chamfer and gouge cuts. The base is shaped from one piece, finished to 10 in. by $3\frac{3}{4}$ in. by 1 in. and is screwed to the case.

DESIGN BY ARNOLD T. BAILEY.

DESIGN BY H. P. NICHOLSON.

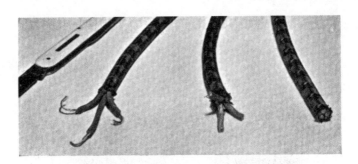

PREPARING THE ENDS OF THE FLEX.

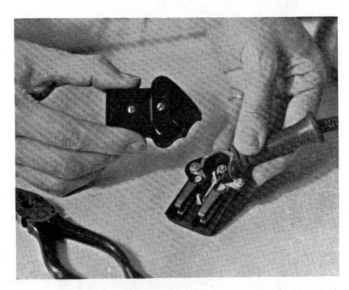

CONNECTING FLEX TO CONNECTOR.

Reproduced by kind permission of The Electrical Development Association.

ELECTRIC IRON REPAIRS

It is very unusual for any portion of the heating element of an electric iron to develop a fault and if it should happen, the iron should be returned to the makers to remedy the defect. With continual use the flexible cable or flex connecting the iron to the socket is liable to wear, or the connections may give way. In the former case it is possible that the rubber insulation may have perished either through old age or over heating, and in the latter case the sudden strain caused by a fall or by the bad habit of disconnecting the plug from the socket by pulling the flex, may either break the wire or pull it away from the connecting screws.

A breakage in the flex may cause a blown fuse, and in this case the position of the fault will, no doubt, be evident, but if the iron fails to get hot when connected up, the plugs at both ends of the flex should be examined. Electric irons are provided with a flexible support at the back which goes far in preventing breakage, but at the other end the flex is usually connected directly to the plug which is fitted into the " point " socket, it is, therefore, advisable to examine this end of the flex first.

Unscrew the cap and, if necessary, renew the connection. First cut off the flex as shown in the photograph, and then enough of the fabric covering to expose sufficient wire to make the new connection. Scrape off the rubber and binding with a sharp knife, but take great care to avoid cutting the wire. The exposed ends of wire are twisted and bound clockwise round the screws, which are carefully tightened up.

If the breakage is on the connector, as shown in the photograph, take off the cap and proceed as for a plug, but it will be seen that a sufficiency of insulated wire must be freed in order to provide enough to wind it over the pins inside. When assembling do not forget the flexible support.

KNOTS AND SPLICES

The commonest form of knot is the overhand or thumb knot, it is extremely easy to tie and never slips when the ends have been tightly pulled. The slip knot illustrated at the top of the next page is not the usual form but it has the advantage of staying " put." The reef knot is a simple way of joining two pieces of string or rope together; it is used for a large number of purposes, but care must be taken to make quite sure that the looping is quite correct. A similar knot used by weavers is made by crossing one of the ends and passing it under the loop, it is particularly strong, and in many cases preferable to the simpler reef knot. The fisherman's knot is suitable for fine cord, when tied it is strong and neat.

The sheep-shank is used when a rope requires to be shortened without being cut. The sheet knot is similar to the weavers' knot and is used for temporary purposes.

Two particularly useful knots are those known as the timber hitch used in scaffolding and in places where the weight will keep the hitch tight, and the fisherman's bend, which is useful where there is a give and take motion or a varying strain on the rope.

Two forms of simple splicing are shown at the bottom of the page. It will be seen that the eye splice consists in threading the ends of a loop in a rope through the separate strands above, each strand being carried over a strand and under alternately. A short splice used to unite two ropes permanently is carried out in the manner shown in the diagram. First of all tuck in the strands from the left hand rope into the right hand rope. The splicing is continued similarly to the eye splice; when the left hand side is done, tuck in the right hand strands in the same way and when completed hammer carefully to close up the strands.

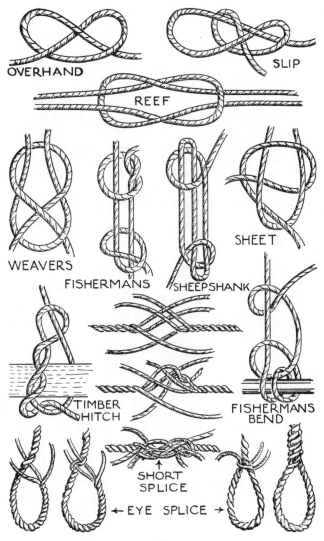

OVERHAND

SLIP

REEF

WEAVERS

FISHERMANS

SHEEPSHANK

SHEET

TIMBER HITCH

FISHERMANS BEND

SHORT SPLICE

← EYE SPLICE →

57

BOOKBINDING

The diagrams on the next page show three stages in sewing the sections of a book together. First of all provide the sewing frame, a simple form of frame shown at Fig. 1 can be folded flat when not in use; the bottom board should measure about 12 in. or so long by 9 in. or 10 in. wide, it need not be more than $\frac{3}{4}$ in. thick. It is advisable to stiffen the board by screwing on end battens of $1\frac{1}{2}$ in. by $\frac{3}{4}$ in. wood. The screw-pivoted upright pieces at the ends should measure a little more than the width of the bottom board and the top piece should fit across as indicated; these pieces should be cut from $1\frac{1}{2}$ in. by $\frac{3}{4}$ in. wood.

Arrange all the sections to be sewn in the correct order, the first section being on top.

To begin sewing, place the first section on the board and arrange lengths of bookbinders tape (about $\frac{1}{2}$ in. wide) as at Fig. 1. Approximately the spaces at each end and between the tapes should be equal. Suitable lines can be drawn on the back. The actual sewing is shown at Fig. 2, and consists of passing the needle and thread from one end to the other in the manner indicated, loops being formed to include each tape in turn.

A second section placed on top of the first is sewn to the tapes in the same way. A third section is similarly dealt with, but before a fourth section is sewn the thread is carried through the loop between the first and second sections, as at Fig. 3. When the end of the third section is reached, the loose end left at the beginning of the stitch should be tied securely to the loop above, as indicated, and the same catch of the loop below should be made before the next section is sewn. Continue in this way until the whole of the sections are completed, when the end of the thread should be tied to the loop below. All the threads should be drawn tightly, if this is not attended to some of the sections will be loose.

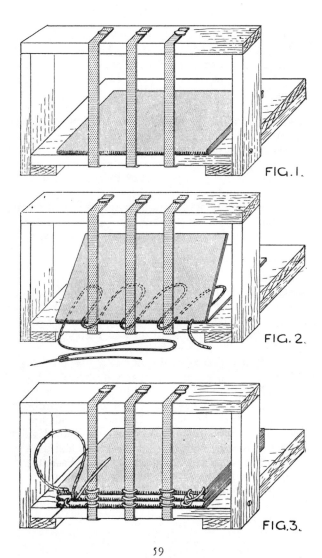

FIG. 1.

FIG. 2.

FIG. 3.

BOOKBINDING II

After the sections of the book have been sewn together as shown on page 59, the edges should be trimmed. A useful form of press for the purpose is shown at Fig. 4, it consists of two lengths of planed wood about 18 in. long and at least 2 in. by 1½ in. in width and thickness. Two ¼ in. diameter bolts with wing nuts should be fitted. For a cutting tool use an old steel table knife broken off straight and sharpened to a keen edge. A 1 in. chisel also forms a useful cutter. The book is screwed up in the press with the edges projecting about ⅛ in. so that sufficient paper is left for trimming as indicated.

If a number of books are to be bound, or the craft of bookbinding is taken up as a hobby, it would be found an advantage to purchase a simple cutting apparatus. The plou plane shown on page 64, obtainable from Dryads of Leicester, is admirable.

Having trimmed the edges the back can be placed directly on the back of the case, but it is an advantage to paste strips of muslin either under the tapes as shown at Fig. 5, or cover the back and tapes with a wider strip of the same material, as shown in the photograph on page 64.

Next fold a piece of stiff paper as at Fig. 6 and paste it to the back, but previously place the book in the press and slightly round the back with hammer. Prepare the cover as indicated at Fig. 7, making the cardboard a little larger than the page. Various materials are available for the back, such as bookbinders cloth, leather or fabric. Paste the covering on the inside and then place the book in position as shown at Fig. 8. Paste the tapes to the cover and then fit in two end papers as shown at E.P., (i) the outside pieces are pasted on the cover as at E.P. (ii) and then place the book under pressure to allow paste to dry.

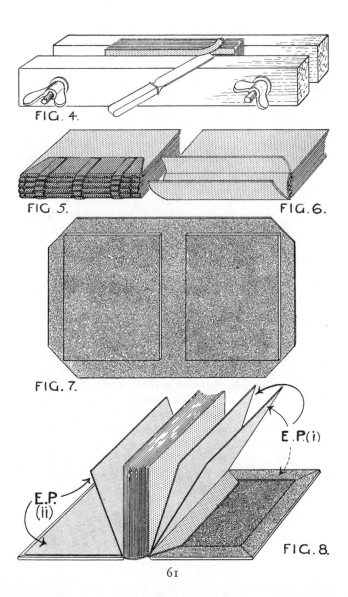

FIG. 4.

FIG 5.

FIG. 6.

FIG. 7.

E.P.
(ii)

E.P.(i)

FIG. 8.

61

COVERING FOR BOOKS

Bookbinders cloth, obtainable in a wide range of qualities and colouring, is inexpensive and is easily attached to cardboard with ordinary paste. Most convenient is the paste powder used by paperhangers, it is obtainable in small packets and needs only to be stirred into cold water.

In pasting cloth, care must be taken that both cloth and cardboard, or preferably strawboard, are thoroughly coated with paste. In pressing the cloth close to the board, always work from the centre to the outside so that all surplus paste is excluded.

Fabrics such as casement cloth make excellent covering for the cardboard case, but considerable care is needed when pasting any woven material. Brown paper is also a suitable material for an inexpensive cover.

Home made cover papers can be made in several ways, one is by means of paste, coloured with a dry powder pigment. Four examples of paste decoration are shown on page 63. The method is to coat some plain paper with colour and allow it to dry. Now mix up some contrasting or harmonising colour with paste and cover the paper evenly. In the top left example, a brush has been drawn through the paste. In the second example at the top the effect is obtained by short strokes of a stiff brush. The third example (bottom left) is patterned with a notched piece of card or a portion of a comb. The remaining example is a pattern formed by a similar comb swung round on one corner. Other interesting cover papers can be made by spreading prepared liquid colours on thin size and placing an absorbent paper on top so that it lifts up the colour. Make the size with powder glue. Thin out artists oil colour with turps. Drop a spot of each colour on the size at intervals, allow it to spread and then draw a skewer through the colours to give a marbling effect.

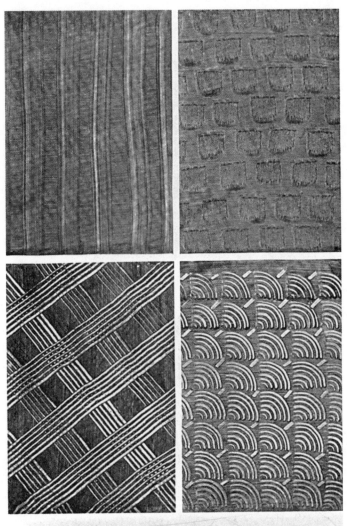

Reproduced by kind permission of Dryad Handicrafts.

PLOU PLANE *by* DRYAD HANDICRAFTS.

THIS PHOTOGRAPH SHOWS THE SEWN BOOK READY
FOR ATTACHING TO THE COVER AND A BOOK
AWAITING THE ATTENTION OF THE HANDYMAN.

CARE AND REPAIR OF BOOKS

Books are liable to damage in many ways, loose and torn leaves, unsightly creases on the page corners, bruises on the corners of the case, stained and torn covers and backs. Generally the damage is preventable, especially in the case of " dog ears." It is always advisable to provide a book-mark for each book. The corner creases when they do exist can be taken out by damping the paper and pressing with a warm iron.

Torn and loose pages can be repaired by using transparent gummed strip, obtainable at a stationers or music sellers. Loose sections can be fitted in place by applying a fine line of seccotine along the back of the section, pressing it into place and placing the book under pressure.

Bruised corners of cases can be stiffened up by moistening them and applying pressure with a warm iron. If they are torn it is advisable to bind them with a narrow strip of cloth or thin leather. If the case is badly damaged as in the example on page 64, the best plan is to cut off the back as carefully as possible and peel off the outside covers in stages to avoid cutting the tapes or strings. A new case made as shown on page 61, with new end papers provided, should be completed as described. In dealing with a very old book, when impossible to make use of the tapes, scrape the back clean, glue on a wide strip of stout muslin and bind as before.

Faded cases can be freshened up by washing with diluted glaire and coated when dry with thin shellac varnish. Leather covered books can be lightly wiped over with a cotton wool pad moistened with olive oil. If soiled, wash over with diluted oxalic acid solution and when wiped off rub carefully with oil. Loose portions of the covering can be fastened with seccotine.

SIMPLE BOOT AND SHOE REPAIRS

It is not a difficult job for the handyman to carry out simple repairs to heels and soles. A few tools are required, a combination last shown at Fig. 1 is quite inexpensive, a shoemaker's hammer (Fig. 2) is convenient but is not essential. A sharp knife should be provided, the most suitable shape is shown at Fig. 3. In addition a rasp should be provided.

In dealing with a leather heel, the best way is to cut out the worn portion as shown at Fig. 4, fit in a suitable piece of leather, cutting it roughly to shape. The kind of rivet used, as shown to an enlarged scale at Fig. 5, should be provided in several sizes. No. 17 gauge iron rivets will be required for the heel; several rows of rivets can be used.

The leather should be wetted and hammered to harden it and then it is riveted in the way shown at Fig. 6. A double row of rivets should be added when hard wear is expected, especially in children's boots. Trim off the edges with the knife, kept as sharp as possible by using an emery-cloth hone. Clean up with a rasp, smooth and coat the edge with heel ball rubbed on with a hot iron.

Half soling is carried out as shown at Fig. 7. First strip off the worn sole and prepare a new sole as shown at Fig. 8. Thoroughly wet and hammer the leather, pare off the waist, pack a thin layer on the old sole if necessary, and then attach the new sole as at Fig. 9 with brass rivets. Trim edges as for the heel. A convenient form of pliers is shown at Fig. 10. A method of preventing wear by attaching protectors is shown at Fig. 11. Boot protectors may be obtained in various shapes and sizes, they are easily hammered on. This diagram shows a rubber heel in position; these are obtainable in several sizes, if not the exact shape, trim with a sharp knife.

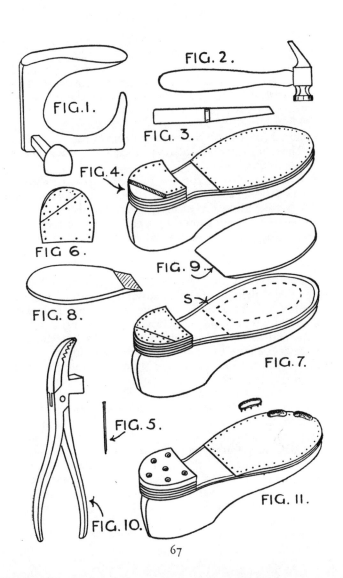

FIG. 1.

FIG. 2.

FIG. 3.

FIG. 4.

FIG 6.

FIG. 9.

FIG. 8.

S

FIG. 7.

FIG. 5.

FIG. 10.

FIG. 11.

RENEWING A FUSE

The replacement of a " blown " fuse is one of the many little jobs that the handyman may be called upon to do. Although it is a simple operation to pull out the carrier and fit a new length of wire in position, it is also necessary that the cause of the fusing should be discovered. When the fuse box is fitted, it is usual for the lighting authority to supply the correct gauge of wire required to carry all the current likely to pass through it.

The authority will always advise as to the correct gauge to use.

It is not unusual for the fuse wire to snap through deterioration, caused either by corrosion, or by continual use having altered the fusing point of the wire ; but also a short circuit caused by a faulty flex connection, or overloading due to additional lamps or elements connected on to the particular circuit, will " blow " the fuse wire.

The first step in mending a blown fuse is to turn off the main switch, open the fuse box and remove the carriers one at a time until the faulty one is located. The old wire should be removed by undoing the screw clips and the porcelain wiped clean. Take a length of wire of the required gauge and fit it in position. There are many patterns of carrier, but the principle of the wiring is the same, it is necessary to secure the ends of the wire at each end of the carrier. The wire should not be stretched tightly or screwed up too firmly. Always replace the carrier before the main switch is turned on. It is important that the cause of the fusing should be known, and if it is caused either by damaged flex or faulty connections, these should be remedied before re-connection to the circuit. It is also a good plan to label in some convenient way the various carriers in the fuse box so that time can be saved in locating a particular circuit.

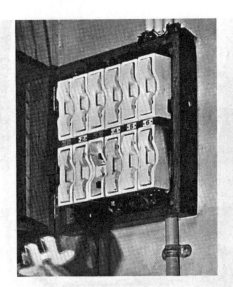

A TYPICAL FUSE BOX.

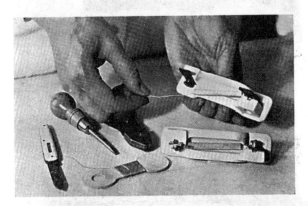

FITTING A NEW FUSE WIRE.

*Photos reproduced by kind permission of The Electrical Development
Association.*

PREPARING PLUG TOP PRIOR TO CONNECTING FLEX.

TIGHTENING TERMINALS OF PLUG TOP.

CONNECTING FLEX TO PLUG TOP.

Photos reproduced by permission of The Electrical Development Association.

FLEX CONNECTIONS

By paying due regard to the efficiency of the connections, extra lighting may be arranged from any existing point; except in the case of portable fires, etc., it is inadvisable to carry out permanent wiring with flex, the correct form of cable should be provided, and as far as possible it should be cased in metal or wood.

In all cases of new connections, special attention should be paid to the capacity of the cable or flex. A flex suitable for a lighting point would be insufficient to carry the current consumed by more than one heating unit. For example, a lighting circuit of 5 amps. would be quite inadequate for a heating circuit of 15 amps.

It is important that the plug and socket fittings should be of good quality. At one time expensive, it is now possible to obtain practically all the necessary material for either a lighting or heating system at a price giving satisfaction in cost and quality.

The accompanying photographs illustrate the tools required and the method to be followed in connecting the flex to a plug. The flex should be prepared as shown on page 54, and then the screws of the plug terminals unscrewed sufficiently to receive the wire.

In connecting the flex just sufficient wire should be bared to wrap round the terminals, but careful note should be taken of the length of covered wire required to fit inside the plug. The screws should be tightened up firmly but not unduly so. In wiring up new lamps from an existing ceiling socket, care should be taken that no undue strain should be placed on the wiring. If a glass shade is fitted, it is generally advisable to support it separately and not allow it to become a strain on the lamp socket; this is a frequent cause of trouble, especially when the lamp has been in use for some time.

It is not economical to use cheap flex, the best quality is always more satisfactory in use.

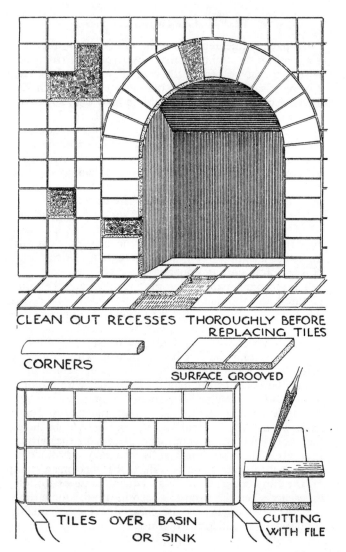

CLEAN OUT RECESSES THOROUGHLY BEFORE
REPLACING TILES

CORNERS

SURFACE GROOVED

TILES OVER BASIN
OR SINK

CUTTING
WITH FILE

73

CUPBOARD AND BOX LOCKS

Generally the only parts of a lock liable to break are the springs which keep the lever tumblers in position. To renew a spring or make any internal adjustments in a simple lever cupboard lock similar to that shown at Fig. 1, remove the box or case as shown at Fig. 2. In the cheaper locks, projections on the edge of the box are riveted to the plate, shown separately at Fig. 3, and should be prised open. In locks of best quality the locks are screwed to the plate. Remove the bolt (Fig. 4) and place it on one side as at Fig. 5. Examine the lever (Fig. 6) and the spring (Fig. 7). New lock springs can be obtained from any ironmonger. The key shape at Fig. 8 is so arranged that the lever is lifted up just enough to allow the bolt to be moved from side to side. In replacing the parts, see that they are all perfectly clean, and touch all pivoting points with oil or paraffin.

Box locks are usually made with two or more levers, a typical example is shown at Fig. 9. First remove the box as indicated at Fig. 10, and it will be seen that the two levers shown at Figs. 11 and 12 are provided with small springs. There is also a bolt as at Fig. 13. All these parts are held together by pegs attached to the back plates as indicated at Fig. 14. Care must be taken to replace springs of correct size and shape and, in replacing the parts, to begin with the bolt which rests over the key pivot, then the levers in turn.

Careful study of the wards in the key will show the position of the levers. It will be seen that the key shown at Fig. 13 will lift the levers just enough for the projection on the bolt to pass through the slots.

New keys can be made from suitable blanks. Failing one for a pattern, the wards on the key can be discovered by examining the levers and cutting the recesses one at a time, using a thin ward file.

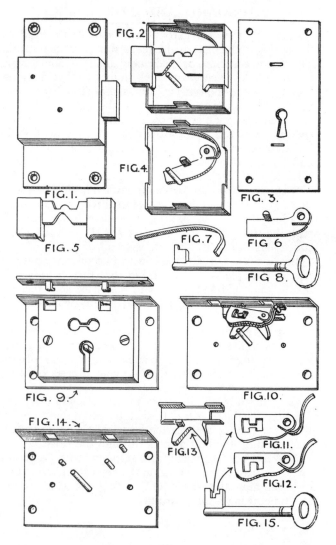

FIG. 2

FIG. 1.

FIG. 4.

FIG. 3.

FIG. 5

FIG. 7

FIG 6

FIG 8.

FIG. 9.

FIG. 10.

FIG. 14.

FIG. 13

FIG. 11.

FIG. 12.

FIG. 15.

75

MORTISE LOCKS

Door locks are usually of the mortise type, but as the mechanism of all doors is similar, the example shown on the next page may be taken as typical of them all. As the springs of locks may snap or sometimes the wards of the key break off inside the lock, the lock must be taken off to effect the necessary repairs. In the case of old locks, it is advisable to clean them thoroughly instead of trying to oil them through the keyhole.

First remove the handle as at Fig. 1, using a bradawl or fine screwdriver to loosen the screw. Next remove the plate, Fig. 2, placing the studs carefully on one side, and then the long screws. If it is difficult to draw the lock from the mortise, push the bolt out, and hold it with pincers, the case can usually be drawn out in this way without trouble. In the case of very old locks which have become rusty, it may be necessary to tap the plate with a hammer, a series of light taps will generally suffice and allow the case to be drawn out.

The cover plate generally is fixed on with a single screw stud as at Fig. 4, and when unscrewed the plate can be lifted off to expose the inside as at Fig. 5. The collet at Fig. 6 should be taken out and the springs examined and, if necessary, renewed; note carefully the springs (T.S.) attached to the tumblers and the stronger one (P.S.), usually a double spring which presses against the plate P. The coiled spring usually secured to the latch has a long life and rarely has to be renewed. The case stripped of all movable parts is shown at Fig. 7. All the parts should be wiped clean with an oily rag and replaced in the reverse order of removal, the positions being indicated by dotted lines. In the event of a broken key, blanks of the correct size can always be obtained and the wards can be cut with a hacksaw and finished smooth with a fine ward-file.

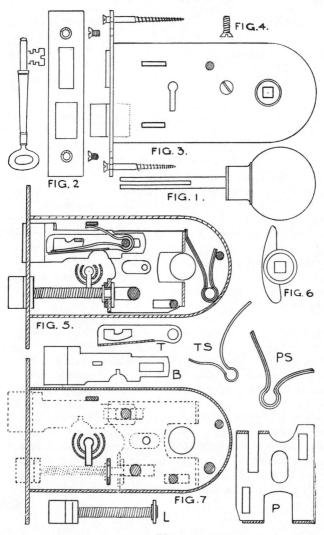

FIG.4.

FIG. 3.

FIG. 2

FIG. 1.

FIG. 6

FIG. 5.

T

TS

PS

B

FIG.7

L

P

CUTLERY REPAIRS

The handyman may be called upon to carry out minor repairs to articles of cutlery. One of the most common is that of the table knife, when the blade becomes separated from the handle. This is actually a simple repair. First scrape all the old cement from the tang and clean out the hole in the handle with a fine drill. Fill the hole in the handle with finely powdered resin or a cement such as Stixit, heat the tang if resin is used, and insert it into the hole. The same method applies in regard to a fish knife or fork, but in this case the space inside the band should be filled also with cement. When the tang of a knife has broken off, the portion left in the handle must be removed and this may prove a difficult job; a fine drill carefully inserted will bore a hole sufficiently deep into the tang to enable it to be withdrawn. The tang should be brought up to its normal length by inserting a piece of iron as indicated, and securing it with solder. The soldered portion should be filed down evenly and then inserted in the handle in the manner stated above. Care should be taken that the hole in the handle is deep enough.

Another likely job is the spring guard of a carving fork. In this case the trouble is caused by the failure of the spring. The rivet securing the guard should be driven out with a fine punch, the hole cleaned out and the old spring examined and renewed. It will be necessary to provide a new rivet from steel wire when replacing the spring.

Bent prongs of table forks may be straightened out by a few light taps with a hammer on the face or edge of a flat iron. With badly bent prongs it may be necessary to prepare a die by filing suitable holes in the edge of a length of iron bar as indicated; the prongs should be hammered lightly into the grooves.

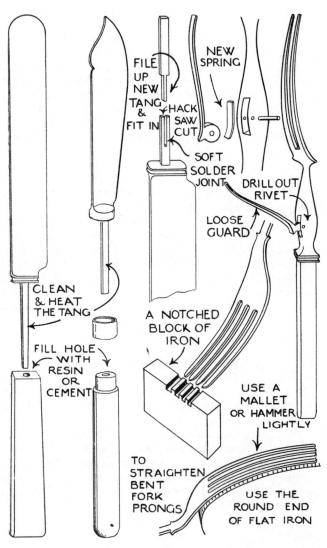

FILE UP NEW TANG & FIT IN

NEW SPRING

HACK SAW CUT

SOFT SOLDER JOINT

DRILL OUT RIVET

LOOSE GUARD

CLEAN & HEAT THE TANG

A NOTCHED BLOCK OF IRON

FILL HOLE WITH RESIN OR CEMENT

USE A MALLET OR HAMMER LIGHTLY

TO STRAIGHTEN BENT FORK PRONGS

USE THE ROUND END OF FLAT IRON

GARDEN TOOL REPAIRS

The first sign of wear in a garden spade or fork usually shows itself in the handle ; when the wood begins to split the fissures may be filled up with plastic wood. If it is necessary to fit a new grip, the end of the centre rod should be filed off and removed as at Fig. 2 and 3. A new grip can be made as at Fig. 4 from a length of round wood as at Fig. 5. With care the end of the old rod can be riveted up again, if not it will be necessary to obtain a new one, or a length of iron rod which can be riveted over washers at both ends. New handles (Fig. 6) can be obtained, these are riveted to the shaft.

In the event of a fracture in the shaft, a good plan is to bind it with strong cord or wire as shown at Fig. 7. Straight grips as shown at Fig. 7 are fitted on, when necessary, with the wedged mortise and tenon joint as at Fig. 8.

New handles are not difficult to fit. In the first place file off the old rivets, shape the end of the new shaft to fit as at Fig. 9 and then fit and fix new rivets as at Fig. 10. The face of a flat iron makes a good anvil for the job.

Rakes with broken prongs are easily repaired, new prongs can be made from stout wire nails filed to fit as at Fig. 11 and riveted in place.

Broken hose pipe can be joined up with a length of brass tubing notched as shown at Fig. 12, and bound round securely, preferably with wire as at Fig. 13.

Garden shears should be sharpened on the bevelled edge indicated by S at Figs. 14 and 15. Use the coarse side of a carborundum stone and follow the method suggested for scissors.

As all garden tools are liable to rust, repairs can often be avoided by paying a little attention to them when not in use. Rub them over from time to time with a vaseline rag.

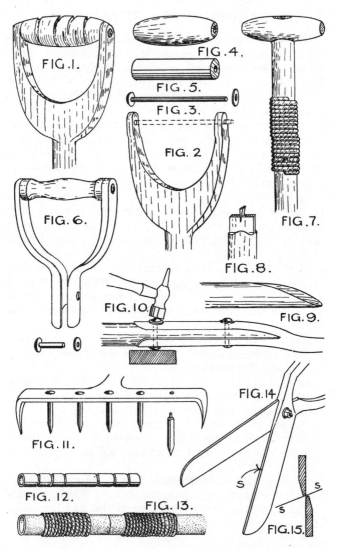

FIG. 1.

FIG. 4.

FIG. 5.

FIG. 3.

FIG. 2.

FIG. 7.

FIG. 6.

FIG. 8.

FIG. 10.

FIG. 9.

FIG. 11.

FIG. 14

FIG. 12.

FIG. 13.

FIG. 15.

s

s

s

PARTITIONS

Dividing partitions for large rooms are not difficult to erect. A typical example is shown at Fig. 1, with an enlarged portion at Fig. 2. For a strong partition on which beaver board, plaster board or plywood can be secured, it is advisable to use 4 in. by 2 in. wood. A lighter partition can be made by 2 in. by 1½ in. wood, but it is inadvisable to use anything slighter.

Begin by cutting off a length to fit exactly from one side to the other and divide this length into approximately 2 ft. spaces, this will allow for 4 ft. wide boards, obtainable 6 ft. and 8 ft. long. Due allowance should be made for the door opening, preferably at one end, but to avoid waste care should be taken to allow for as many 4 ft. widths of board as possible.

Having decided on the position of the uprights, mark off the grooves in the top piece and from these marks set out the bottom piece. The end uprights are butted against the wall with allowance for the skirting and are fitted under the top plate. The ends of the bottom plate fit against the end uprights.

When the top and bottom plates are ready, the door post and cross bar prepared, erect in the required position previously marked by guide lines. Test by plumb line and then screw to floor and nail to joists. Fit in studs and secure with nails driven in on the skew, prepare the nogging pieces and nail on as shown.

The framework is now covered and finally the door opening should be lined and architraves fitted. An easily made door is shown at Fig. 3, using 2 in. by 1 in. wood, a brace of 6 in. by ¾ in. board and a covering of plywood. Hinge with strong butts and provide a door stop of 1 in. by ½ in. wood on the opening side of framework. A temporary partition can be made in the same way and covered with canvas instead of boards.

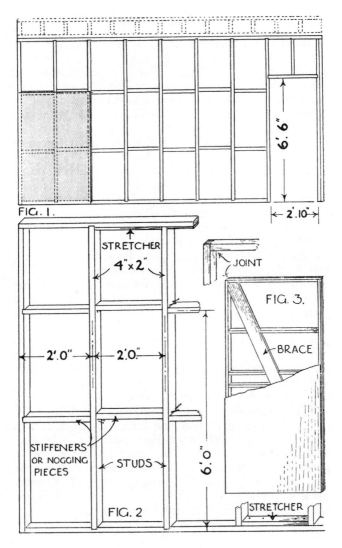

FIG. 1.

6' 6"

2'.10"

STRETCHER

4"x 2"

JOINT

FIG. 3.

2'.0"   2'.0"

BRACE

STIFFENERS
OR NOGGING
PIECES

STUDS

6'.0"

FIG. 2

STRETCHER

PANELLING A ROOM

By the use of oak faced plywood and prepared strips of oak, effective panelling as shown at Fig. 1 can be carried out in any room. The necessary plywood can be obtained in 5 ft. lengths, but for heights of 6 ft., lengths of 4 ft. and 2 ft. can be used. It is possible to attach the plywood to the wall direct, but as this entails the removal of the skirting, it is better to prepare a foundation framework first as shown at Fig. 2, using ordinary deal battens which need not be planed down, providing they are sawn to size.

In arranging the uprights of the framing, the standard widths of plywood should be taken into consideration ; they are 24 in., 36 in., and 48 in., the uprights, therefore, should be so placed and spaced that they coincide with the joins. The horizontal bars, H.B., are grooved to take the uprights V.B., and both uprights and bars equal in thickness to the skirting, should be secured to the wall with rawlplugs.

First nail on all the plywood, working from corner to corner, as shown at P on the next page, and then prepare the oak strips which should be from $1\frac{1}{2}$ in. to 2 in. wide and $\frac{1}{2}$ in. thick as indicated at Fig. 3. In Fig. 2, S.R. shows the short rail, W, the skirting, R the long rails and C the capping ; the latter being about 2 in. by $\frac{3}{4}$ in.

In the sectional diagram at Fig. 4 R.P. represents the rawlplugs used in attaching the foundation bars to the wall, W, the new skirting, R, the rails, and C, the capping. A suggestion is given at D for short round plugs of hardwood to be fitted in countersunk screw holes ; there is, however, no necessity for the plugs because oval brads can be used to secure the strips. If the heads of the brads are driven in below the surface and the hole filled in with plastic wood, they will not be noticed. Reference should be made to the instructions given on page 158 for finishing the surface.

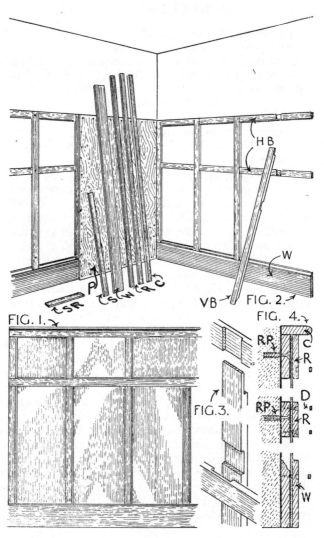

HB

W

P

SR S W R C

VB FIG. 2.

FIG. I.

FIG. 3.

FIG. 4.

RP C R

RP D R

W

85

PLYWOOD WALL COVERING

Two modern treatments of plywood panelling are shown on the next page, both being in complete contrast to the traditional panelling shown on page 85. In carrying out the scheme illustrated in the upper photograph, Venesta oak panelling was used, the floor and furniture being of birch.

A foundation framing similar to that shown on page 85 should be fixed to the wall in the first place, but as Venesta can be obtained in lengths to fit between the floor and ceiling, a slight variation will be needed. Ordinary deal battens 3 in. by 1 in. are suitable, a rail should be fitted close to the ceiling, with two or more rails equally spaced between. The vertical battens should be spaced so that the joins in the panelling occur on one of the uprights.

The lengths of the panelling should be fitted very carefully; some slight adjustment with a plane may be necessary to fit the panel to the floor, but care must be taken that the vertical line is retained.

As the effect of the panelling should not be marred by using nail marks, it is advisable to use fine panel pins. Hammer marks must be avoided and a fine nail punch should be used to drive the pins just below the surface; the small nail holes thus made should be filled with plastic wood or other suitable filling, stained to the colour used in the finishing process.

The panelling of Sapele mahogany on the lower photograph shows the possibility of using long and comparatively narrow strips of plywood with chamfered edges placed horizontally. In this case it will be necessary to have the vertical members of the wall framing much closer together than needed when vertical panels are used. With Venesta panelling, it is possible to apply a wax polish without further preparation of the surface or the use of glasspaper.

VENESTA OAK PANELLING.

VENESTA SAPELE MAHOGANY PANELLING
CHAMFERED.

THE ENTRANCE HALL OF A SMALL MODERN HOME
BEFORE TREATMENT OF THE FLOORS AND
WOODWORK.

AN UNTOUCHED PHOTOGRAPH OF THE SAME HALL
AFTER TREATMENT WITH COLRON STAIN AND RONUK.

Reproduced by kind permission of Weldons Ltd.

FLOOR STAINING

The secret of successful staining is to use a penetrating dye, one that is durable and will drive deeply into the grain. But however good the dye it· will not give satisfaction unless the floor is prepared. It must be quite clean and free from dust.

To begin with go over the boards with a hammer and a nail punch and make quite sure that there are no nail heads projecting above the surface. The surface of the boards should be as smooth as possible, and if there should be any rough portions they should be scraped quite smooth. For this purpose use a handled hook-scraper.

Remove all dust and shavings after scraping with a soft brush. Fill any prominent spaces between the boards with plastic wood, if they are wide it will be advisable to fill with thin strips.

If the floor has been stained before it is an advantage to remove as much of the previous stain as possible by scrubbing with sugar soap, but do not neglect to wash away all traces of the soap. A scraper can be used to finally clean up the surface.

A suitable and reliable stain is Colron, it should be applied with a wide brush or with the special tool available for the purpose. Pour the stain into a bowl, wipe the brush on the side after dipping, and then rub the stain on the wood just as quickly as it is absorbed. Do not use too much for the penetrating power of the stain is considerable. Leave it to dry for about twelve hours.

Rub it down with a dry cloth and then apply Ronuk evenly, rubbing it well into the surface and leave it for an hour or two to dry. Wax polishes should be applied with a fairly stiff brush and finished with a soft cloth. It is better to rub a little thoroughly on the surface than to apply it thickly.

TAKING UP FLOOR BOARDS

It is not always a simple matter to take up a floor-board, particularly when the boards are tongued and grooved, but there are occasions when the handyman is called upon to carry out the job. In taking up a particular section of the boarding it may be necessary to cut a board. In this case one of the simplest ways is to cut a series of holes with a bradawl as indicated at Fig. 1. If the holes are made between the joists, sufficient space to allow the insertion of a padsaw blade is all that is needed; but when the cut is made over a joist, a complete row of holes quite close together will be necessary, the remaining fibres being severed with a sharp chisel. The nails of the board, beyond the place required, should be driven down with a nail punch into the joist.

The next step consists of prising up the board by using two chisels or a chisel and screw driver, with small blocks of wood as shown at Fig. 2. The necessary length of board should be sawn off to a bevel with a tenon saw, the end being supported by a strip of wood as shown at Fig. 3. In replacing the board the straight end should be supported on a block nailed underneath as indicated at V in Fig. 4; the sloping end as at S will hold firmly.

When the boards are tongued and grooved, the tongue can be sawn through with a pad saw as indicated at Fig. 5. Another method is to use two screw eyes as at Fig. 6, form a loop with wire and then lever the boards up.

A recess for a mat is prepared in the above manner, the required recess in the joist should be cut out with a chisel and the boards replaced as shown at Fig. 7. In this diagram it will be seen that one end of the board at A is not long enough to fit against the joist as at B. Care should be taken to gauge the thickness of the block at A to give the required depth.

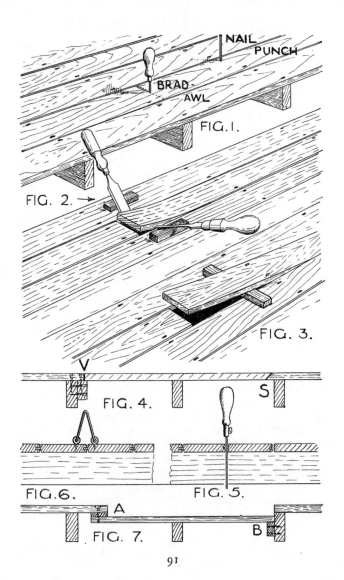

FIG. 1.

BRAD-AWL

NAIL PUNCH

FIG. 2.

FIG. 3.

V

S

FIG. 4.

FIG. 6.

FIG. 5.

A

B

FIG. 7.

LEAKAGES IN TAPS

All taps, especially those which are provided with washers, are liable to leak. Apart from the trouble involved in undoing the tap, the renewal of the washer is simple. An ordinary water tap or faucet is shown at Fig. 1, normally it consists of a brass casting, a nut containing a gland, a jumper to which the washer is attached, and the handle. Generally the nut is screwed anticlockwise and this must be remembered when using the wrench or spanner.

The jumper with its washer and nut is shown at Fig. 2. The jumper is easily lifted out when the nut has been removed. The seating should be examined to remove pieces of washer remaining. The new washer, preferably of rubber or composition, should be tightened up and then the jumper and the nut replaced. Leakages at the gland indicates that the packing is defective: replace with string or fibre. The modern type of tap (Fig. 3) is provided with a cap covering the nut, this must be unscrewed and lifted up before the nut can be reached.

The kind of tap shown at Fig. 4, used generally for gas, may leak owing to the presence of grit or liquid. Unscrew the small nut, remove the plug (Fig. 5) and clean thoroughly. Clean also the inside. If the plug is worn, a small portion of the bottom of the plug may be filed off as indicated at Fig. 6. This must be done carefully to prevent damage to the thread.

Leakages in cisterns are generally due to faulty washers at the point shown at Fig. 7. The ball and lever should be removed and a new washer fitted by unscrewing the top of the jumper as shown at Fig. 8.

Leakages in the sink waste are due, as a rule, to a faulty joint or slackness in the screw plug as indicated at Fig. 9. Some string wrapped round the plug before screwing up will usually give a watertight joint.

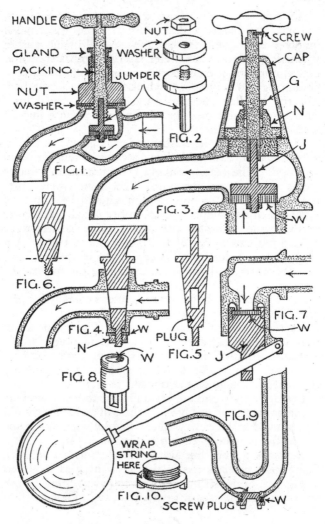

HANDLE

NUT

GLAND WASHER

PACKING JUMPER

NUT

WASHER

FIG. 2

FIG. 1.

SCREW

CAP

G

N

J

FIG. 3.

W

FIG. 6.

FIG. 4. W

N

PLUG

FIG. 5.

J

FIG. 7

W

FIG. 8. W

FIG. 9

WRAP STRING HERE

FIG. 10. SCREW PLUG W

93

DRAIN STOPPAGES

A section showing a typical inspection chamber, an important part of every modern drainage system, is given at Fig. 1. Usually there is sufficient slope to the pipes to carry all the drainage away, but in the event of a stoppage, the chamber should be examined. If it is found that a good flooding of the chamber does not immediately result in a clearance of all deposits, it may be necessary to use a drain rod. In a spell of dry, hot weather it is advisable to flush the drains with a hose pipe. It is sometimes a difficult job to locate the exact position of a stoppage and if a long cane or one of the specially jointed rods made for the purpose does not effect a clearance, it would be advisable to get expert advice.

In the event of a stoppage in the W.C. pan, it is usually a simple job to find a remedy ; the section at Fig. 2 of a typical pan makes the construction clear. Usually a bent cane is sufficient to move the accumulation of paper or other matter, especially as the stoppage is generally caused by the pressure of the water on top being insufficient to force the obstruction into the drain. A plunger as at Fig. 3 may be used if the cane is not effective. A useful tool, shown at Fig. 4, consists of a length of flexible tubing with one or two round knobs secured to the end. Old pieces of flexible tubing should always be kept as the material forms an excellent cleaning rod.

In the event of a stoppage in an outside drain or gulley leading from the sink or bath, it is quite possible that an accumulation of grease on the inside of the trap may cause the trouble. In this case the grease can be removed by using a bent rod as at Fig. 6, but at the same time the gulley must be cleared of sediment at the bottom and thoroughly flushed out with a plentiful supply of water.

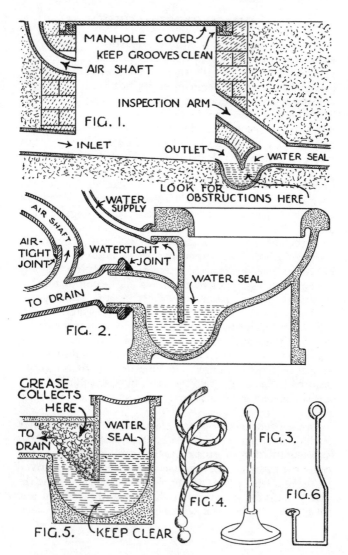

MANHOLE COVER
KEEP GROOVES CLEAN
AIR SHAFT

INSPECTION ARM

FIG. 1.

→ INLET

OUTLET

WATER SEAL

LOOK FOR OBSTRUCTIONS HERE

WATER SUPPLY

AIR SHAFT

AIR-TIGHT JOINT

WATERTIGHT JOINT

WATER SEAL

TO DRAIN

FIG. 2.

GREASE COLLECTS HERE

TO DRAIN

WATER SEAL

FIG. 3.

FIG. 4.

FIG. 6

FIG. 5. KEEP CLEAR

FROST PRECAUTIONS AND REPAIRS

With ordinary care it is possible to avoid burst pipes; wrapping canvas round the exposed pipes is not sufficient, a protective layer of air is necessary. An effective method of protecting pipes from freezing is shown at Fig. 1, it consists of wrapping a generous quantity of clean straw horizontally along the pipe. The straw is covered with strips of thick felt and covered with canvas. Another method is to case the piping in wood, especially if it is in an exposed position. The inside is packed with straw horizontally as at Fig. 2 or any loose material such as paper or old rags.

In dealing with a burst, a temporary method is to close up the opening as at Fig. 4, tapping the sides lightly with a hammer, covering with putty as at Fig. 5 and binding firmly with canvas strip as at Fig. 6. Another method is to cover with canvas and bind with a metal clasp as at Fig. 7.

A permanent repair may be carried out by covering the split with solder or lead as at Fig. 8. First scrape or file the pipe clean, form a recess with plasticine in the way shown at Fig. 9 and pour molten lead or solder into the opening. Clean off the plasticine when the metal is set. When it is necessary to repair a vertical pipe use a bent piece of tin with a surround of plasticine to form an opening for the molten metal as at Fig. 10.

The wiped joint made by the plumber is made by pouring molten solder on the pipe and allowing it to run on to a thick cloth as at Fig. 11. The cloth is pressed against the solder when on the point of setting and twisted round. A join between two pipes is made in the way shown in the section at Fig. 12. It will be seen that one of the lengths is widened out; this can be done with an old bradawl handle driven in gently or by the revolving of a round rod. The other length is filed down to fit.

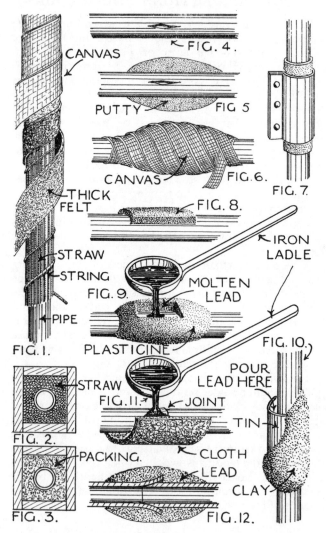

CANVAS

FIG. 4.

PUTTY

FIG 5

CANVAS

FIG. 6.

FIG. 7.

THICK FELT

FIG. 8.

IRON LADLE

STRAW

MOLTEN LEAD

STRING

FIG. 9.

PIPE

PLASTICINE

FIG. 10.

FIG. 1.

POUR LEAD HERE

STRAW

FIG. 11.

JOINT

TIN

FIG. 2.

PACKING.

CLOTH

LEAD

FIG. 3.

FIG. 12.

CLAY

INTERIOR PAINTING

The most important item in painting is the quality of the paint. Cheap paints are generally unsatisfactory and are not economical either in use or wear. It is advisable to obtain ready mixed paints made by well-known manufacturers.

First of all the surface to be painted must be perfectly clean, all cracks and nail holes should be filled with putty. In the case of new wood paint cover all knots with one of the preparations sold for the purpose, and cover the surface with a good undercoat. All good paint manufacturers have a medium suitable for the purpose.

When preparing a painted surface for a new coat wash it down thoroughly. Mangers sugar soap is excellent for the purpose, but take care that all the soapy water is rinsed off and the surface quite dry before the new paint is applied.

Next to the paint and the preparation of the surface in importance is the brush. It is advisable to use two rubber-set brushes as at Figs. 1 and 2. One, about 2 in. wide, and the other narrow, about $\frac{3}{4}$ in. or 1 in. Flick them with the fingers to remove dust before use. As it is important to keep the paint stirred every few minutes, it is therefore necessary for this purpose to have a stick as at Fig. 3.

When applying the paint, work from the top downwards holding the brush lightly and firmly as shown at Fig. 4. When painting large surfaces use a wide brush and apply the paint in parallel lines, joining the lines as indicated at Fig. 5, and then finish with vertical strokes with the brush.

The best method of painting a door is shown at Fig. 6. Begin with the panels and then follow in the order indicated. It is always better to apply two thin coats of paint carefully, rather than one thick coat.

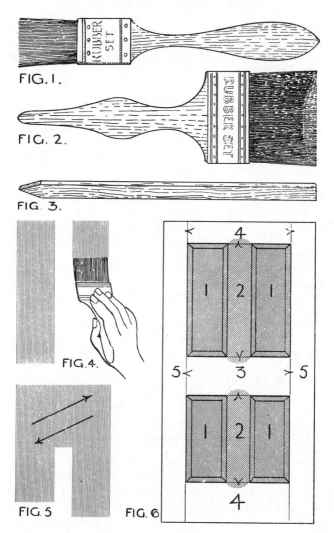

FIG. 1.

FIG. 2.

FIG. 3.

FIG. 4.

FIG. 5

FIG. 6

EXTERIOR PAINTING

The same instructions for interior painting apply to exterior work, but usually much more care is needed in the preparatory work. Owing to the action of the weather, outside paint work is liable to blister and peel; in this case it is essential that all the old paint should be removed. In order to save time and trouble this important part of the preparation is sometimes neglected, but with the aid of a blow lamp and a scraper, or by the use of some of the well-known brands of liquid paint remover, no difficulty is likely to be experienced. In either case it is advisable to wash the cleaned surface before a new coat of paint is applied; this is especially important when a chemical remover is used. Surfaces that have not blistered can be rubbed down with pumice stone.

It is advisable to have a hog hair brush (Fig. 1) for getting into difficult corners. A sash tool (Fig. 2) is useful for sashes and small work, and one or two large brushes (Fig. 3) must be provided. The paint should be used from a handled tin (Fig. 4) using the S hook when working from a ladder. Stretch a wire across the tin so that surplus paint can be stroked off the brush without waste. When the brushes are not in use they can be kept in a jar containing turps as indicated at Fig. 5. When painting sashes it is advisable to use a shield of cardboard or tin as indicated at Fig. 6.

Outside iron work should be rubbed down with a wire brush, two forms being shown at Fig. 7. It is also useful to have an old knife (Fig. 8) and as well, an old file will be found very useful. Repairs to railings should be carried out before painting, some suggestions for simple repairs are shown at Fig. 9. Outside paint work should not be done during wet weather or in hot sunshine; follow the sun in spring and autumn and the shade in summer.

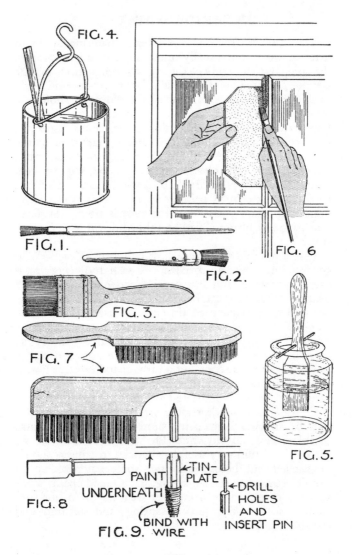

FIG. 4.

FIG. 1.

FIG. 2.

FIG. 3.

FIG. 6

FIG. 7

FIG. 5.

FIG. 8

PAINT
UNDERNEATH

TIN-
PLATE

DRILL
HOLES
AND
INSERT PIN

BIND WITH
WIRE

FIG. 9.

WHITEWASHING AND DISTEMPERING

Whitewash can be made by mixing whiting and size in water, but it is more convenient to use a preparation mixed ready for use. Limewash is a mixture of slaked lime and water and is generally used for out-buildings. Distemper is a paint available in a great variety of colourings and may be obtained washable, non-washable and mixed with water or oil.

As a rule neither whitewash or distemper should be applied unless the surface on which it is to be placed has been washed down very thoroughly and is dry. The plaster should be examined carefully and any cracks or holes filled up with plaster of paris. Care should be taken to smooth down all rough places. It is an advantage to coat the whole surface with size after cleaning unless an oil-bound distemper is being used.

When applying whitewash or distemper, use a large brush and hold it in the way shown on the next page. Keep the mixture in the bucket well stirred, and for economy stretch a wire across the top of the bucket so that surplus liquid can be stroked off the brush.

In dealing with a ceiling it is advisable to carry out the work in stages as indicated in the diagram, and in the case of papered walls to be left untouched, large sheets of newspaper should be pinned to the picture rail to prevent any splashes. If the room is a large one, work from side to side.

A pleasing finish can be imparted by the use of a stipple brush. First apply the distemper with a flat brush and then apply a second coat with the stippler. This method gives an even finish free from brush marks, but care should be taken not to overload the brush.

A suggestion is given on the next page for an easily made trestle. With one of these, a ladder and a long board or two, large surfaces can be covered quite easily.

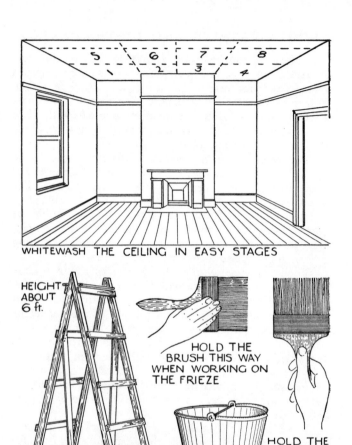

WHITEWASH THE CEILING IN EASY STAGES

HEIGHT ABOUT 6 ft.

HOLD THE BRUSH THIS WAY WHEN WORKING ON THE FRIEZE

HOLD THE BRUSH THIS WAY WHEN WORKING ON THE CEILING

$2\frac{1}{4}" \times 1\frac{1}{4}"$

EASILY MADE TRESTLE WITH TOP SHELF TO HOLD PAIL.

STRETCH A WIRE ACROSS THE PAIL

PALETTE & KNIFE FOR USE WITH PLASTER

PLASTIC PAINT FINISHES

Plastic finishes are a very popular method of decoration and, although generally they require the services of a craftsman, simple designs are within the scope of the handyman.

The accompanying illustrations show the method of producing a simple texture suitable for a bathroom or kitchen. Plastic paints may be obtained in powder form which, mixed with water, forms the paint, or as a ready mixed paint bound with oil or spirit varnish. Either variety may be tinted to suit the scheme of decoration, certain of the oil bound materials do not require further decoration.

To obtain a plastic finish apply the paint with a large brush, 2 in. in size or over ; a substantial layer (No. 1) being applied without particular care in application. Before the paint has set, a stippling brush, similar in shape to a shaving brush is dabbed over the surface to produce the effect shown at No. 2. Alternatively the brush may be twirled on the paint, giving a surface as shown at No. 3. If the surface is to be painted, the plastic must be allowed to dry and the paint applied in the ordinary way. If the top spots are wiped before the paint is dry, a two colour scheme is obtained. One oil bound plastic paint does not require painting, a pleasing effect being obtained by drawing a steel scraping knife over the surface when the paint is almost set ; this flattens out the top spots giving flat spots with rough designs interspersed (No. 4).

When the plastic is hardening off, a vigorous rub with a cloth produces a high lustre on the top flat surfaces and gives the effect of polished marble with dull markings interspersed.

Some plastic paints dry hard and do not chip and, furthermore, are resistant to moisture and alkali thus rendering them particularly suitable for bathrooms and kitchens.

FIG. 1.   FIG. 2.

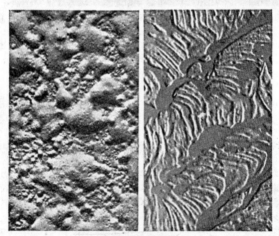

FIG. 3.   FIG. 4.

*Reproduced by kind permission of
Modern Paints & Finishes Ltd.*

AN EXAMPLE OF PLASTIC DECORATION ON AN
EARTHENWARE POT.

PLASTIC PAINT DECORATION

Apart from wall finishes, plastic paint may be used with pleasing effect to decorate articles of furniture and to transform otherwise worthless articles into decorative features for the house. The illustration on the previous page shows how a stained and chipped earthenware pot can be turned into something of value and artistic appearance.

To produce this effect, clean down the pot thoroughly with medium glasspaper, remove the dust and dry the surface. Apply a coat of good priming paint which will help to satisfy the porosity of the material and also form a good key for the plastic paint. When the undercoat is thoroughly dry, apply the plastic in the way described on page 104, moulding the surface to the structure desired. The particular effect illustrated was obtained by rough stippling, first with a cream and then with a reddish brown, the high spots being smoothed off. Mottled effects may be obtained by dabbing with a stencil brush dipped in various colours and the edges of the colours wiped into each other with a soft rag.

Another effect can be obtained by placing some gold powder in a bag made from an old silk stocking, the powder is shaken over the half dry paint. Plastic paint lends itself to innumerable decorative effect, particularly for friezes, panels, imitation medallions, firescreens, etc. With the aid of a brush and a pointed stick, large flower forms such as roses, chrysanthemums, peonies, dahlias can be modelled and painted. The possibilities of plastic paint render it an excellent medium for the handyman with a *flair* for decoration.

FIXING CEILING BOARDS

It is often more economical to repair a damaged ceiling with prepared boards than to strip off the old plaster and re-plaster, a difficult job for the inexperienced amateur to attempt; in any case all loose plaster should be removed before the boards are fixed in position, but better still, the whole of the plaster should be removed, although it is a troublesome and dusty job.

Ceiling boards are available in two forms: one is composed of wood pulp and fibre, the other of wood pulp and plaster, in both cases the boards are formed by compression. Standard sizes run from 6 ft. to 16 ft. long and from 3 ft. to 4 ft. wide. Fibre boards are made in two thicknesses, $\frac{3}{16}$ in. and $\frac{1}{4}$ in., but the plaster board is $\frac{3}{8}$ in. thick and heavier. Both kinds of board are easy to saw, but plaster boards are more difficult to handle owing to their greater liability to break. Nails and screws can be used on both types of board.

A plan of the ceiling should be drawn out on paper to a suitable scale, with the position of the joists accurately indicated. A careful selection of standard sizes should be made in order to save undue cutting and waste. Assistance will be necessary in placing the boards in position, but the position of the boards can be maintained while they are nailed to the joists by using the means shown at Fig. 1. The same sketch illustrates a panelled effect produced by battens nailed on to the joists and covering the joints. It is advisable when using fibre boards that they should be fixed in position with a gap of $\frac{1}{4}$ in. between, to allow for expansion, as indicated at Figs. 2 and 3. With plaster boards this allowance is not necessary for the edges can be butted together, any spaces being filled with plastic cement. Plaster board ceilings treated in this way can be distempered and papered. Fibre board ceilings can be finished with paint.

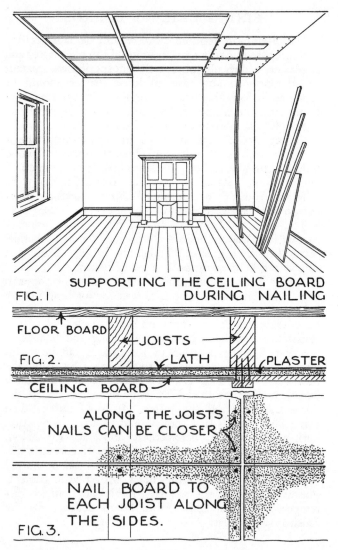

SUPPORTING THE CEILING BOARD
DURING NAILING

FIG. 1.

FLOOR BOARD

JOISTS

FIG. 2.   LATH   PLASTER

CEILING BOARD

ALONG THE JOISTS
NAILS CAN BE CLOSER

NAIL BOARD TO
EACH JOIST ALONG
THE SIDES.

FIG. 3.

RENEWING SASH CORDS

The first job in renewing a broken sash cord is to take out the front sash. It will be seen that the sash is kept in position by means of a bead, known as the staff bead. A portion of this beading must be pulled out as shown on the next page. A wide chisel is a convenient tool to use, but a screwdriver can be driven in behind the bead on the inside to avoid marks on the front. The front sash is now lifted out and placed on a chair under the window. If the breakage is on the top sash, it will be necessary to remove the parting bead dividing the two sashes in the same way.

To get at the weight, look on the side of the frame for the pocket piece, open it by driving in a bradawl to use as a handle and then pull out the weight. Remove the ends of the cord from the weight and note carefully the way it is attached. Pull out the nails securing the cord to the sash and then cut off a new length of cord to the same length as the broken pieces placed together.

As it is rather troublesome to thread new sash cord through the pulley, the usual method is to use a length of string having a small weight at one end, this is called a mouse. Insert the mouse, which need not be more than a narrow strip of lead attached to the string, tie the end of the string to the new cord and draw it out through the hole. Tie the end of the cord to the weight and then fasten the other end to the sash with clout nails. The sash is now lifted carefully into place.

After testing, the pocket piece and the parting bead, if removed, should be tapped in place and finally the staff beads replaced. In the latter case the nails should be driven back before the beads are sprung into position.

It is generally advisable to renew all the cords when one of them breaks.

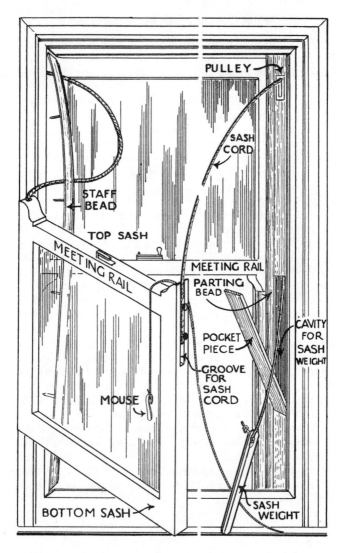

PULLEY

SASH CORD

STAFF BEAD

TOP SASH

MEETING RAIL

MEETING RAIL

PARTING BEAD

POCKET PIECE

CAVITY FOR SASH WEIGHT

GROOVE FOR SASH CORD

MOUSE

SASH WEIGHT

BOTTOM SASH

III

NEW PANE OF GLASS

First of all pull out all the broken portions of the glass, then clean out the rebate and remove completely all the old putty. In the case of a window recently re-glazed, the removal of the comparatively soft putty is a simple matter, but with old putty, it will be necessary to use a chisel or knife similar to that shown at Fig. 2. If the putty is very hard the help of a hammer will be needed, but some care will be required to avoid cutting into the wood. Do not be content to just cut out the putty but scrape it all off to expose the wood.

Measure the size of the opening and cut the glass to size; it should fit in with no more than $\frac{1}{16}$ in. play. The next job is to line the inside of the cleaned rebate with well-worked putty; when newly purchased the putty should be rolled out and worked between the palms of the hands until it ceases to crumble. Small bits should be placed in position on the rebate pressed in and spread evenly. The glass is now placed in position and pressed on the sides with the fingers and thumb spread widely apart, until it is bedded down. On no account press on the centre of the glass. The outside is now covered with putty, pressed carefully in position and then smoothed down as indicated in the diagram with a putty knife (Fig. 3). Finally cut off the surplus putty found on the inside of the rebate.

Thin window glass can be cut quite easily with a wheel glass cutter as shown at Fig. 4. Hold the cutter upright and firmly, press evenly and break off the glass by resting it on the edge of a bench or a table as indicated at Fig. 5.

In dealing with leaded lights the broken glass is removed by levering up the flange of the lead with a putty knife. Cut the new piece to shape and fit in position and press the lead smooth again. It may be necessary to solder the joint.

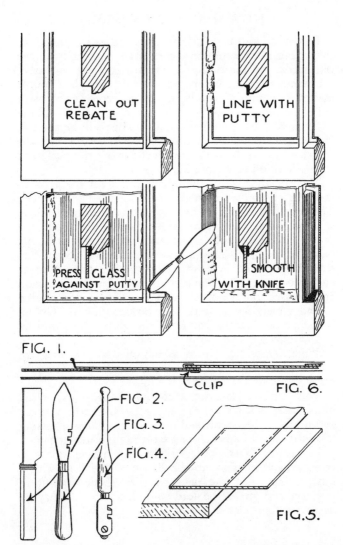

CLEAN OUT REBATE

LINE WITH PUTTY

PRESS GLASS AGAINST PUTTY

SMOOTH WITH KNIFE

FIG. 1.

CLIP   FIG. 6.

FIG. 2.

FIG. 3.

FIG. 4.

FIG. 5.

113

EASILY MADE LADDERS

The handyman who wishes to carry out repairs himself will need at least one ladder, preferably two; for in this case with a plank long enough he will be able to reach ceilings for whitewashing and papering. There is an additional advantage, if, however, the ladders are so made that one can be joined to the other. For example with two 7 ft. ladders, a height of 12 ft. can be reached without difficulty.

The diagrams in the next page give the necessary dimensions for making two 7 ft. ladders so arranged that one forms an extension of the other, while allowing each one to be used separately when required. The ladders may be made longer if desired, but the method of construction is the same.

The construction of ladders is quite simple. For one provide four lengths of deal, as free from knots as possible, measuring 7 ft. by 3 in. by 2 in. Place the four lengths and mark off a line 7 in. from the bottom. Now set out 9 in. spaces along the remainder of the length. Place two of the lengths 18 in. apart at one end and 16 in. apart at the other and draw lines across from side to side. Place the other pair 16½ in. apart at the bottom and 14 in. at the top and draw lines across as before. Now prepare 16 lengths of 2 in. by 1 in. wood for the steps and rungs, and cut out notches as shown, these should be marked out with a bevel. Saw down the short line and cut out the waste with a chisel. It will be seen that two of the rungs at the bottom of the narrower ladder are let in flush, to allow it to fit against the wider one.

Nail the rungs securely with two nails in each and then trim the ends neatly to bring them flush with the sides. The metal sleeves should be made of sheet iron or mild steel about ⅛ in. thick to the given sizes, and then screwed on in the positions shown.

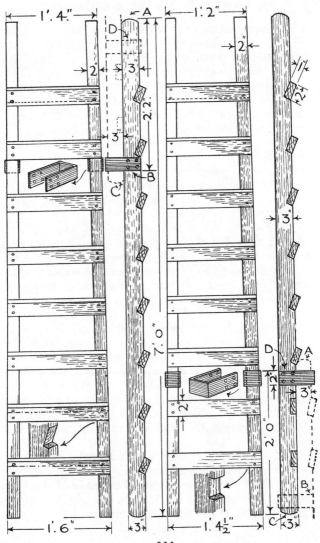

ROOF REPAIRS

Broken tiles and slates should be replaced as soon as possible ; actually tiles are generally easier to replace than slates. A section of a tiled roof is shown at Fig. 1, the tiles rest on rows of battens as shown at Fig. 2, but it is customary to nail every few rows. In the event of a tile being broken it will be necessary to lift up the tiles above. For example to replace the tile A in Fig. 1, the three tiles on the row B must be lifted up so that two tiles on the row below at C can also be lifted up sufficiently to slip the tile A on to the batten. The tiles are let down in the reverse order.

When new slates have to be fitted, the nails fastening the old slates must be cut off with a slater's ripper as at Fig. 3. When the space is clean, prepare a strip of zinc and nail to the batten as at Fig. 4. The new slate is now slipped in position and the zinc strip is folded over as indicated in the sections at Figs. 6 and 7.

In dealing with a felt or rubberoid roof, the best method of making joins in the material is shown at Fig. 8. It will be seen in the side view at Fig. 9 that the overlap is secured with clout nails as shown at Fig. 10. A suitable capping of wood for a felt roof is shown at Fig. 11.

Corrugated iron roofing is secured by nails and bolts as shown at Fig. 12. The capping or ridge used in this form of roofing is shown in the side view at Fig. 13. In fitting new corrugated sheets, the galvanised nail and washer required is shown at Fig. 14 and the nut and bolt, also supplied with a washer, is shown at Fig. 15.

In any case roof repairs are not simple, and in effecting any tile or slate repair, care is needed to prevent more breakages. It is advisable to use a roof board or a light ladder resting on pads made of sacking. Make quite certain that the ladder cannot slip.

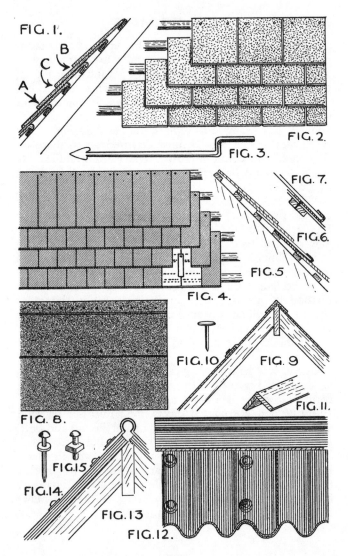

FIG. 1.

B

C

A

FIG. 2.

FIG. 3.

FIG. 7.

FIG. 6.

FIG. 4.

FIG. 5.

FIG. 10.

FIG. 9.

FIG. 11.

FIG. 8.

FIG. 15.

FIG. 14.

FIG. 13.

FIG. 12.

117

NAMEPLATE IN REPOUSSÉ

Of the two forms of lettering suitable for name-plates in copper, brass or pewter, the block letter shown at Fig. 1 is simple, but the Gothic style at Fig. 2 is more attractive.

First decide upon the size of the plate and then space out the letters on paper ; as a rough guide to the height of the letter, divide the length of the line of lettering by the number of letters, allowing for the ends and the spaces between the words. In the example there are 10 letters and 3 extra spaces ; for a plate measuring 10 in., divide by 13, thus the letters will be about ¾ in. high.

Make a tracing of the wording, turn the tracing over, transfer with carbon paper to the back of the plate, which should be about 18 or 20 S.W.G., and then scratch them in with a scriber. Fasten the plate to a piece of wood with drawing pins and then proceed to indent the spaces, with a hammer and a punch, as shown at Fig. 3. The punch should be guided between the lines to obtain a uniform depth as indicated in the section at Fig. 4.

Turn the plate so that the raised letters are uppermost as at Fig. 5, and then trim them up with a tracer to the shape shown in the section at Fig. 6, by the method shown at Fig. 7, using a hammer and tracer. Take care to impart an even width to block letters and graduations to the Gothic letters.

When the lettering is finished drill holes at the corners, polish up the surface with pumice powder applied with a hard brush, and finally coat with colourless lacquer or cellulose finish.

The base should be of oak with the corners slightly chamfered or rounded. Pipe clips can be used if the nameplate is to be placed on a gate or on iron railings. Screw the plate on after fixing the base in position.

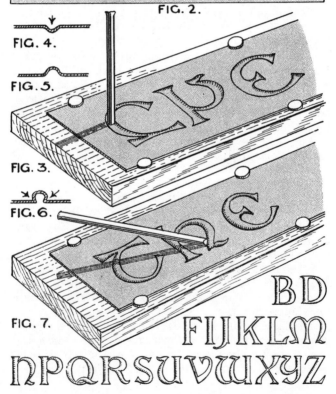

THE COTTAGE

FIG. 1.

THE COTTAGE

FIG. 2.

FIG. 4.

FIG. 5.

FIG. 3.

FIG. 6.

FIG. 7.

BD
FIJKLM
NPQRSUVWXYZ

LAYING LINOLEUM

Care is needed not only in measuring up the floor but also in preparing the surface. It is advisable first to draw a plan of the floor as indicated at the top of the next page. Careful measurements should be made particularly in regard to chimney breasts, bay windows, etc.

The width of linoleum is usually 6 ft. wide and it is generally advisable to lay it in the opposite direction to the floor boards. For the particular room shape given as an example of planning, it happens that two widths of linoleum just take up the length. As far as possible the planning should provide for the material to be laid in pieces as long as possible without undue cutting. With plain colours it is a simple matter to deal with odd spaces, but with patterned linoleum, some waste in matching the pattern is inevitable.

Attention should be given to the floor itself before the linoleum is laid. First of all go over the boards with a hammer and nail punch and make certain that there are no projecting nails. Old floors often show projecting knots, these should be trimmed off with a chisel. If there should be any holes, caused either by dried knots or mice, cover them with pieces of tin as indicated.

Linoleum should be laid on an under layer of felt or brown paper, but in the case of uneven boards and wide spaces, fill up the gaps with thin wood and plane level. An alternative method is to pack the hollow portions with paper.

In cutting linoleum use a special knife and keep it sharp. Work along a chalk line or straight edge. Always allow for expansion and for this reason do not nail it down at once, leave it if possible for a few weeks and then use the special brad indicated. Linoleum may be laid with a special cement ; in this case there is no need to allow for expansion.

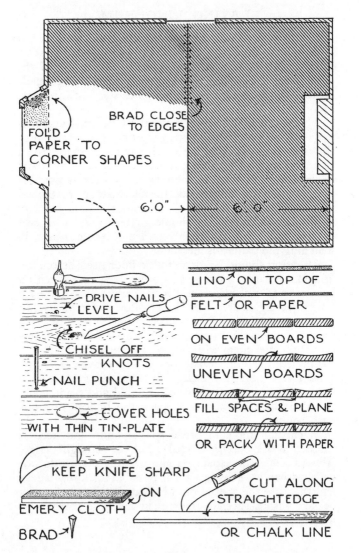

FOLD PAPER TO CORNER SHAPES

BRAD CLOSE TO EDGES

6'.0"   6'.0"

DRIVE NAILS LEVEL

CHISEL OFF KNOTS

NAIL PUNCH

COVER HOLES WITH THIN TIN-PLATE

KEEP KNIFE SHARP

ON EMERY CLOTH

BRAD

LINO ON TOP OF

FELT OR PAPER

ON EVEN BOARDS

UNEVEN BOARDS

FILL SPACES & PLANE

OR PACK WITH PAPER

CUT ALONG STRAIGHTEDGE

OR CHALK LINE

PLUGGING WALLS

The old method of inserting solid wood plugs in a wall to carry a screw or nail is entirely superseded by the invention of the rawlplug, and, instead of unsightly holes in the wall, often unsatisfactory for the purpose, neatness as well as strength is achieved.

All that is required in fixing a rawlplug is a small hammer, screwdriver and the rawlplug tool. (Fig. 1).

The fibre rawlplug is suitable for all ordinary purposes and it is made in a number of sizes suitable for the screws and nails to be used. For example, a No. 3 plug, obtainable in lengths of $\frac{1}{2}$ in., $\frac{5}{8}$ in. and $\frac{1}{4}$ in. and 1 in., will take Nos. 12 and 3 screws and No. 12, 2 in. wire nails. No. 6 plug made in the same lengths is suitable for Nos. 4, 5 and 6 screws, and No. 11 wire nail. A No. 20 rawl-plug, in lengths of 1 in., $1\frac{1}{2}$ in., 2 in., $2\frac{1}{2}$ in., will take Nos. 19 and 20 screws. It is important that the right number and correct length of rawlplug should be obtained. The plug should be slightly larger than the diameter of the screw and as long as the threaded part.

In making the hole, hold the tool as indicated at Fig. 2. Keep the tool straight, tap it lightly with the hammer and turn the tool from time to time. Heavy blows with the hammer may drive the tool in the wall quickly, but it has the effect, especially in a plaster wall, of loosening the plaster and enlarging the hole. Remember to tap lightly and turn. The better the fibre plug fits the hole, the more it will grip and neater it will look.

Fit the rawlplug in the hole as indicated in Fig. 3, then insert the point of the screw into the centre of the rawlplug as at Fig. 4, and turn the screw straight home. Just as soon as the screw tightens up, the fixing is complete.

To prevent mistakes in using the wrong kind of plug it is advisable to state, when purchasing plugs, exactly the kind of fixing required.

FIG. 1.

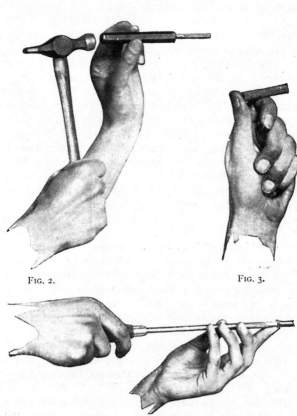

FIG. 2.   FIG. 3.

FIG. 4.

HOW TO USE RAWLPLUGS.

Wireless aerial fixed to brick.

Fixing guttering to brick.

Fixing hand-rail to brick.

Fixing capping and casing to plaster.

Lavatory basin and piping fixed to plaster

Geyser, gas and water piping fixed to tile.

PHOTOGRAPHS OF VARIOUS RAWLPLUG FIXINGS.

MODERN FIXING

A number of typical fixing jobs are illustrated on the opposite page, if rawlplugs are used they can be carried out by the handyman with ease and a knowledge of perfect security. There are rawlplugs for every kind of screw, and special white bronze plugs designed for outdoor jobs. For heavy fixing use rawlbolts.

In fixing into brickwork it is more satisfactory to drill the hole into the brick and insert a rawlplug, than to drive a wooden plug into the joint. This applies to all kinds of fixing jobs when brickwork is involved. Do not force the tool, simply tap and turn.

When fixing to soft plaster, it is advisable to use a Bullet Bit for making the hole and pierce by giving the rawlplug tool holder careful blows with a hammer of medium weight; in this case do not rotate between the blows. Should the articles to be fixed be at all weighty it is advisable not to trust to the plaster but to drill right through it into the brick beyond.

In fixing to tiles and glazed bricks, it is necessary to remove the glazed surface over the area required for the rawlplug; this can be done by holding the tool in the hand and rotating forward and backward under steady pressure. Special tile drills, for the purpose, can be obtained.

When dealing with lath and plaster walls use a long rawlplug, turn the screw into it to the extent of about $\frac{1}{4}$ in., being careful to grip the plug tightly to ensure it does not split the whole of its length. The plug and screw is then inserted into the wall, the swelling caused by the insertion of the screw will grip the sides of the hole and the screw can be turned home satisfactorily.

The ordinary drill can be used for making holes in the harder varieties of marble, slate and stone, but for the softer kinds the best results are obtained by using a twist drill.

WINDOW BOXES

The measurements for a window box should be made as shown at A in Fig. 1 and at B in Fig. 2 ; the inside depth should be about 6 in. In the simple form of box shown at Fig. 3, the front board should be wider than the back ; support underneath should be provided by pieces as at A. Suitable decoration can be given by strips of $\frac{1}{2}$ round wood as at B, arranged as indicated at Fig. 4 or in any suitable pattern.

Another method of treating the front is to cut out suitable shapes in thin wood and brad them to the surface as shown at Fig. 5. The front board may be shaped by recessing a portion of the edge or by working in a curve. The design at Fig. 6 indicates the possibilities when using straight lines. In all cases the joints should be nailed securely.

A pleasing shape for a box is shown at Fig. 7 ; in this design the end pieces are nailed to the front and back pieces with the decorative strip bradded on. Suitable shapes for a plain box with curved front edges are given at C and D in Fig. 8.

It is necessary in all window boxes to allow for drainage, Fig. 9 shows a suitable method of planning the drainage holes, which should be about $\frac{3}{4}$ in. diameter.

Another shape for a window box is shown at Fig. 10 with a half-plan showing drainage holes at Fig. 11. The end boxes may be so arranged that they project beyond the sill, the centre portion should be long enough to fill the space shown at A in Fig. 1.

Methods of securing window boxes as shown at Fig. 12 ; angle brackets can be attached to the box and window frame, or iron plates can be screwed to the ends of the box and fixed to the wall as shown at C. The inside of the box should be coated with melted pitch and the outside painted with three coats of paint.

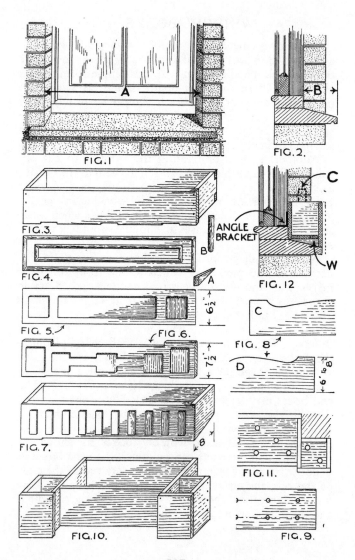

FIG.1.

FIG.2.

B

FIG.3.

FIG.4.

B

A

FIG.5.

FIG.6.

6½"

7½"

FIG.7.

8

FIG.10.

FIG.8.

C

D

6" to 8"

ANGLE BRACKET

C

W

FIG.12.

FIG.11.

FIG.9.

127

PREVENTING DRAUGHTS

The admittance of fresh air into a room is important, but it need not cause discomfort. One of the frequent causes of draught is a badly fitting door. A simple means of preventing an under-door draught is to fit a felt or rubber covered roller as at Fig. 1. The brackets are made with a slot as at Fig. 2 to allow the roller to rest on the floor. Another method is to use a folded strip of inner tube as at Fig. 3, or one of the several forms of door draught stop sold for the purpose.

Badly fitting sashes and doors may be dealt with by using prepared strip as shown at Fig. 4. This material can be obtained all rubber as at Fig. 5 or with a wooden moulding as at Fig. 6. When carefully fitted, undesirable draughts can be eliminated.

Draught screens are a convenience, especially when windows or doors are immediately in front of the fireplace. They are not difficult to make and may be designed to provide a decorative feature in the room. Constructional methods are shown at Fig. 9 for a four-fold screen made with a wooden frame and covered with suitable fabric. For this purpose such materials as rexine, tapestry, cretonne and hessian can be used, in the latter case the material can be covered with paper scraps.

The framework of a screen should be jointed together as shown at Fig. 8, the wood need not be more than $1\frac{1}{2}$ in. by $\frac{3}{4}$ in., but it is advisable to use 3 in. wide pieces at the bottom. Additional strength can be given by iron brackets or by corner pieces of wood as shown at A and B. The fabric should be stretched tightly and secured to the edges as at Fig. 9. Another method of dealing with a screen is to panel the frame as shown at Fig. 10. Folding screens can be hinged by using ordinary butts as at Fig. 12, or hinges of leather or webbing as at Fig. 13. Three-way hinges as shown at Fig. 14 are particularly useful.

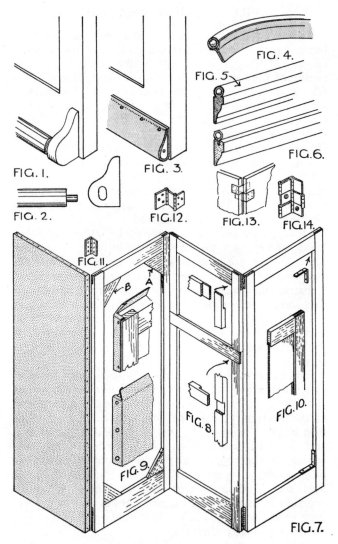

FIG. 1.

FIG. 2.

FIG. 3.

FIG. 4.

FIG. 5

FIG. 6.

FIG. 12.

FIG. 13.

FIG. 14.

FIG. 11.

FIG. 8.

FIG. 9.

FIG. 10.

FIG. 7.

FIRESIDE BOOKSHELF

The sketches on the next page give all the necessary details and dimensions for making a modern type of fireside bookshelf. It may be in deal or whitewood, to be finished with stain or paint, better still in oak requiring only polish as a finish. The material for the sides and shelves can be obtained machine planed to 9 in. wide and $\frac{1}{2}$ in. thick. The back is of $\frac{1}{4}$ in. thick plywood.

Begin with the upright A, this has three grooves marked out as indicated and cut to a depth of $\frac{1}{8}$ in. Care should be taken that the grooves on the inside of the upright B correspond with those on A. The top C fits directly on the top of the uprights A and B. The three shelves at E are made to the same dimensions. The pieces marked F and G fit into grooves in the upright B, and it should be noted that the grooves are stopped within about $\frac{1}{2}$ in. from the front edges in each case. A similar groove is made for the upright H, but the upright piece at S is notched at the bottom only.

With ordinary care in marking out the grooves and the corresponding ends and shelves, there should be no difficulty in carrying out the simple constructional work involved.

The joints should be glued and nailed with fine brads, but the nail heads should be driven just below the surface. Nail on the plywood back not only to the outside edges but to shelves as well, in order to give increased strength. The drawer is shown separately, the front K should be 1 in. thick. The sides and ends need not be more than $\frac{1}{2}$ in. thick. Two methods of attaching the sides L and the back M are shown, the bottom of the drawer should be of plywood. The recessed handle can be cut with a gouge and chisel, it should be screwed on from the inside. If desired the bookcase can be raised from the floor level by a 2 in. by 1 in. frame measuring 22 in. by 8 in. approximately.

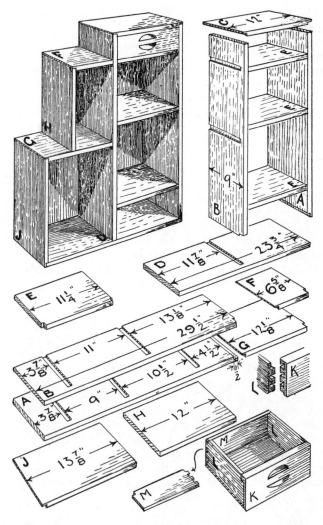

COVERED STOOL

Oak is a suitable material for the construction of the stool shown in three views at Figs. 1, 2 and 3. For the legs provide four pieces each 15 in. by 1½ in. by 1½ in., and plane down to 1⅜ in. by 1⅜ in. For the top rails cut out two lengths 28 in. by 3¼ in. by ⅞ in, and plane to 3⅛ in. by ¾ in. The bottom rails are cut from a piece 3 ft. 6 in. by 1⅛ in. by 1⅛ in., planed to 1 in. square.

The positions of the mortises in the legs are shown at Fig. 4 and the shape of the rails indicated at Fig. 5. Mark out the exact length of the shoulders leaving ⅞ in. as the length of the tenons. The top inner edge of each of the top rails is rebated ½ in. wide and as deep as the thickness of the plywood, which has to be fitted on as shown at Fig. 6.

Care should be taken in marking and cutting out the mortises in the legs, this being done before the curves are worked to shape with a spokeshave. It will be seen that the shaping occurs on the two outside surfaces only. Glue up the joints and use a cramp to pull them together. The plywood top is nailed on.

A simple method of upholstering is shown at Fig. 7, but all staining and polishing should be done before the top is covered in. A piece of Hairlok cut to the shape of the space should be fitted in position. A suitable piece of cretonne, tapestry or leather, large enough for edges to be turned in, is placed over the Hairlok and nailed down. Edging may be used as a finish if desired. Loose hair can be used as a stuffing if desired, but it will be necessary to provide a covering of hessian before the outside cover is attached.

By substituting 2½ in. rails for the shaped rails, and omitting the rebating and plywood top, the stool is made suitable for rush or sea-grass seating carried out as shown on pages 46 and 49.

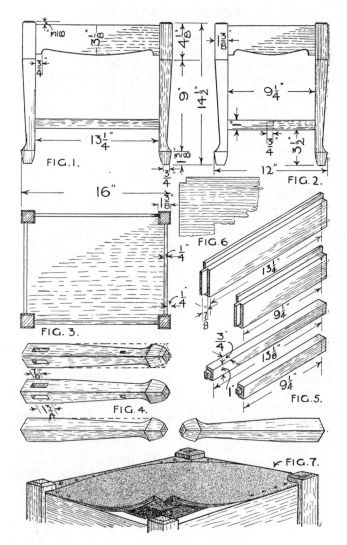

FIG. 1.

FIG. 2.

FIG. 3.

FIG. 4.

FIG. 5.

FIG. 6.

FIG. 7.

VEGETABLE RACK AND TABLE

The design at Fig. 1 shows an easily made form of vegetable rack combined with a useful small table. The dimensions can be varied to suit individual requirements, but it will be found that a height of 30 in. to 32 in., a width of 18 in. or so and a depth of 14 in. will be a convenient size.

Begin the construction by making the two uprights as at Fig. 2, with $\frac{3}{4}$ in. deal or tongued and grooved boards to a width of $13\frac{1}{2}$ in., and cut to a length of $31\frac{1}{4}$ in. Nail on a 3 in. by 1 in. strip at the bottom with a slot 2 in. by 1 in. for the bottom front rail. The next strip 1 in. by 1 in. should be screwed on to leave a space of 8 in. above the bottom piece. Two more strips are screwed on, leaving spaces of 7 in., 6 in. and $3\frac{3}{4}$ in. at the top. The sides are joined together at the bottom by a $14\frac{1}{2}$ in. length of 2 in. by 1 in. wood, at the top by an 18 in. by 14 in., projecting $\frac{1}{2}$ in. in front and 1 in. at the sides, and at the back with a piece of plywood. Some 2 in. wide moulding as at Fig. 3 should be nailed on the bottom. The top drawer at Fig. 5 is $3\frac{3}{4}$ in. deep, the front piece is 1 in. thick, sides and back $\frac{1}{2}$ in. thick and the bottom plywood.

The drawers below are made with solid sides joined by $1\frac{1}{2}$ in. by $\frac{1}{2}$ in. strips as at Fig. 6. They should fit easily without side play. The width and depth is the same in each case, $14\frac{1}{2}$ in. by $13\frac{1}{2}$ in., the heights are 8 in., 7 in. and 6 in. respectively. The side flaps of the table top are the same width as the top and cut to 9 in. or 12 in. long; hinge them to the top piece with butt hinges and fix iron brackets, as at Fig. 4.

A suitable finish is white or cream cellulose finish. Begin with an undercoating of white and allow it to dry. Do not apply a second coating of cellulose finish until the first coat is quite hard and has been rubbed down with pumice or worn glasspaper.

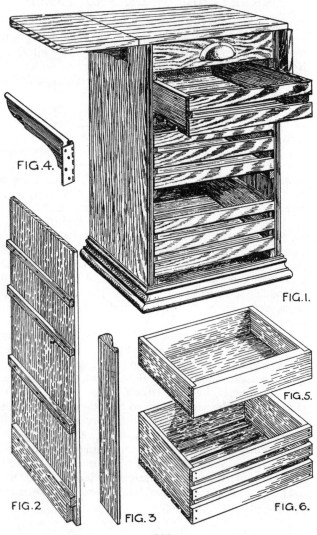

FIG. 4.

FIG. I.

FIG. 2.

FIG. 3

FIG. 5.

FIG. 6.

GROCERY CUPBOARD

This cupboard is designed to hold sixteen 3 lb. glass jars and from six to eight tins. The two sides and inner shelves are made from 5 in. by $\frac{3}{4}$ in. wood, the uprights being 24$\frac{1}{2}$ in. and the shelves 24$\frac{1}{2}$ in. long. Prepare four strips 5 in. by 1 in. by 1 in. and screw them on to the inside of the uprights, the top of the lower strips being 7$\frac{1}{4}$ in. up from the bottom and the top edge of the other pair are 7$\frac{3}{4}$ in. above.

Join the sides together at the top with two 26 in. by 1$\frac{1}{2}$ in. by $\frac{3}{4}$ in. pieces let into notches, with a piece similar in size across the front as shown at Fig. 2. The bottom board shown at Fig. 3 measures 27$\frac{1}{2}$ in. by 6$\frac{1}{2}$ in. by $\frac{3}{4}$ in. Grooves 5$\frac{1}{4}$ in. long and $\frac{1}{4}$ in. deep are cut to take the uprights, the distance between them being 24$\frac{1}{2}$ in. Fit the board in position and screw it from underneath. The back is of $\frac{1}{4}$ in. plywood and measures 26 in. by 24 in.

Cover the top with a 30 in. by 8 in. length of plywood, and then cut 1$\frac{1}{4}$ in. lengths from a 2 ft. length of 1$\frac{1}{4}$ in. Scotia moulding shown at Fig. 4. Glue these blocks underneath the projecting top as at Fig. 1, spacing them approximately $\frac{1}{2}$ in. apart; the pieces at the corners should be mitred.

The two doors are made from $\frac{1}{4}$ in. thick plywood, each piece measures 22$\frac{1}{2}$ in. by 13 in., this should be checked by the size of the opening. The plywood is faced with strips prepared to 1$\frac{1}{2}$ in. by 1$\frac{1}{2}$ in., formed into a framework as at Fig. 5. The corners should be glued and screwed together and the framework glued and screwed to the plywood, care being taken that the corners are square. Fit on a cupboard knob and turn as at Fig. 6, and either a ball catch or a bolt as at Fig. 7. Finish with paint or stain and polish. As the cupboard will be heavy when fitted, it will be advisable to support it on iron brackets fixed to the wall underneath and attach mirror plates at the top.

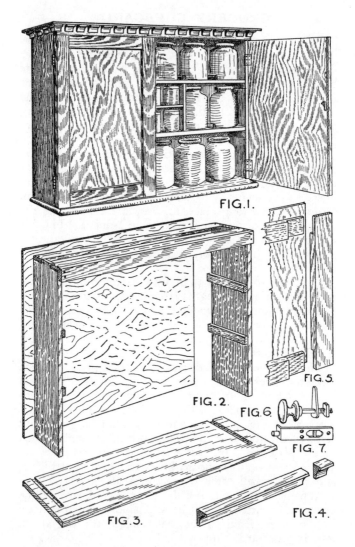

FIG. I.

FIG. 2.

FIG. 5.

FIG. 6.

FIG. 7.

FIG. 3.

FIG. 4.

PAPERHANGING

Before papering a wall strip off the previous paper. Thoroughly wet the wall and peel off the paper with a scraper (Fig. 1). Next examine the wall for cracks and if necessary fill them up with plaster, using the scraper or a putty knife (Fig. 2) and leave the surface smooth.

Provide a large pair of scissors (Fig. 3), a good quality pasting brush (Fig. 4), and also a paperhanger's brush (Fig. 5). In estimating the number of rolls required, a simple method is to find how many times one roll, which measures 21 in. wide, will go completely round the room and divide by four. The dealer will, no doubt, trim the paper on a machine.

The paper should be cut into the required lengths, due allowance being made if there is a pattern to be matched. Place the paper face downwards on a board or table covered with newspaper. Make some paste by pouring sufficient cold-water paste-powder into a bucket or bowl and mix thoroughly. Paste one strip completely and fold the ends over as shown.

Care must be taken that the first piece is hung quite straight, hang a plumb line from the picture rail and mark the wall as a guide. When the paper is straight as at 1, Fig. 7, smooth it down with the brush from side to side to press out surplus paste and air bubbles, paying particular attention to the top and bottom. Stroke the scissors along the skirting and the rail to obtain a close fit as at 2, cut off the waste, and brush the paper again close up against the wall as at 3. In hanging the second and following pieces see that the cut edge is correctly spaced on the next piece as shown at Fig. 8, and that the pattern coincides exactly. Begin and end at the least conspicuous corner of the room, usually behind the door. Portions under the windows may be left until last, but usually it is better to follow on strip by strip.

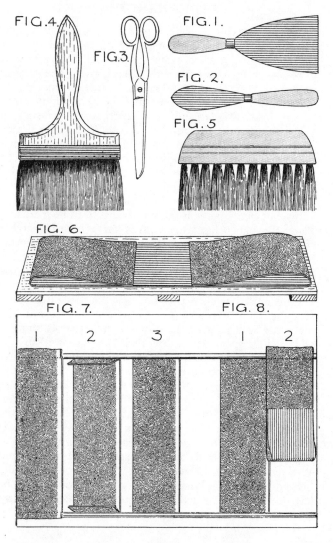

FIG. 4.   FIG. 3.   FIG. 1.

FIG. 2.

FIG. 5.

FIG. 6.

FIG. 7.   FIG. 8.

1   2   3   1   2

PAINTING FURNITURE

As it is possible to purchase white wood furniture inexpensively and as much of the ready-to-assemble furniture prepared for the handyman to put together is also in whitewood, it is necessary to know something about suitable methods of finish. Although the ready-made or ready-to-assemble articles are generally sent out with a good surface, it is always worth while to rub down the surface again.

The method of cellulose finish is described on page 158, the same procedure should be followed in using enamel paints. There is, however, another and particularly effective way to paint whitewood or deal furniture, suitable for new or old articles ; this is illustrated in the frontispiece and is known as " combing." The four suggestions indicate some of the possibilities of the process and any two colours which blend well or give good contrasts can be used.

Decide on the two colours ; those used in the frontispiece, for the purpose of reproduction, give strong contrasts. The first or bottom colour will be the one which will appear when the second colour is combed. The comb, obtainable in varying thicknesses of teeth or spurs, can be made from celluloid or thin metal sheet or purchased separately or in sets and is quite inexpensive.

Use ordinary oil colour and apply the first colour in two coats or one coat will do on a suitable undercoat. It is advisable to rub the surface down when quite dry with powdered pumice applied with a thick piece of felt. Wipe the surface clean and then apply the second colour. Now the comb is brought into use and it will be found that the scrolled and wavy patterns are the most successful. Keep the comb clean by wiping it after each stroke.

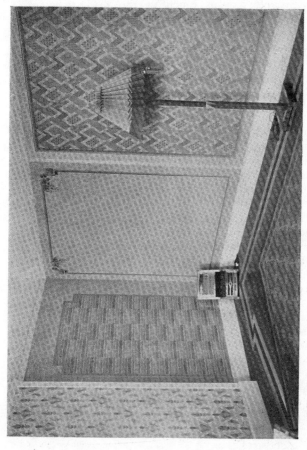

FOUR SPECIMENS SHOWING MODERN APPLICATIONS OF WALLPAPER.

(By courtesy of Messrs. H. E. Olby & Co.)

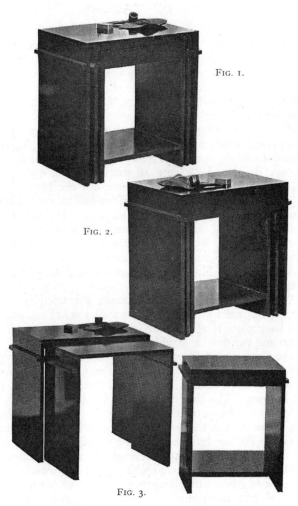

FIG. 1.

FIG. 2.

FIG. 3.

AN EASILY MADE NEST OF TABLES.

NEST OF TABLES

A compact nest of tables forms an extremely useful piece of furniture. The photographs on the preceding page shows a nest of three tables, all convenient in size and particularly strong yet most simple in construction. Figs. 1 and 2 illustrate the front and back views of the tables packed together and in Fig. 3 the three pieces are separated.

To save jointing, it is advisable to use American whitewood, machine planed $\frac{3}{4}$ in. thick. For the largest table cut off two uprights 1 ft. $8\frac{1}{2}$ in. and for the top one piece 1 ft. 9 in. long, and all prepared to a width of $14\frac{3}{4}$ in. Prepare a $3\frac{1}{2}$ in. wide strip for the back, two $14\frac{3}{4}$ in. by $\frac{3}{4}$ in. strips for the outsides and two strips the same length but $\frac{1}{4}$ in. wide. Bore holes for screws on the top piece and countersink them, screw on the inner strips 3 in. down from the top edges of the side pieces, screw on the top and fit in and screw on the back piece under the top. Finally screw on the side strips 3 in. down.

The next table is similarly made, the uprights are 1 ft. $7\frac{5}{8}$ in., the top 1 ft. $6\frac{1}{8}$ in. and all 1 ft. $1\frac{3}{4}$ in. wide. The back piece is $2\frac{5}{8}$ in. wide, the inner strips are $2\frac{1}{4}$ in. down and the outside strips $2\frac{5}{16}$ in. down.

The third table has two uprights 1 ft. $6\frac{7}{8}$ in. and a top 1 ft. 3 in. long with widths of 13 in. There are two 2 in. wide strips under the top and a shelf $2\frac{3}{4}$ in. up from the bottom. The side strips are $1\frac{5}{8}$ in. down.

Screw all the parts together, the countersunk holes will allow of the screw heads being driven below the surface. Fill up hole with plastic wood, and clean all the surfaces with glasspaper, if necessary using a scraper.

The wood is now coated with a prepared wood filler and rubbed down with glasspaper. One coat of cellulose finish should be applied, the example shown is black. When the surface is quite hard, rub down with pumice powder and then apply the final coat.

COFFEE TABLE

The top of this table revolves on a centre hinge attached to the under framing, the latter being shown as a separate detail on the next page. If possible use oak, and prepare two uprights $17\frac{1}{2}$ in. by $5\frac{1}{4}$ in. by $\frac{3}{4}$ in., one length $14\frac{1}{2}$ in. by $5\frac{1}{4}$ in. by $\frac{3}{4}$ in. Plane down to 5 in. by $\frac{5}{8}$ in. Cut out two pieces 11 in. by $2\frac{1}{4}$ in. by $\frac{3}{4}$ in., plane to 2 in. by $\frac{5}{8}$ in., and one length $14\frac{1}{2}$ in. by 4 in. by $\frac{3}{4}$ in., and plane to $3\frac{3}{4}$ in. by $\frac{5}{8}$ in.

The joints for the above pieces of wood are shown in a separate detail. First fit the uprights into the feet by means of a double mortise and tenon joint. The tenons should be approximately $1\frac{1}{2}$ in. wide with a corresponding space between and they should be about 1 in. deep. The cross bar at the bottom is tenoned into the feet, in this case the tenon should be about $1\frac{1}{4}$ in. wide and carried right through the footpiece as shown in the side view and details. The top bar is dovetailed as indicated. Care should be taken to mark out the joints as accurately as possible.

The top is made from three lengths finished to $18\frac{1}{2}$ in. by 6 in. by $\frac{5}{8}$ in., but it would be more convenient to use plywood or laminated wood $\frac{5}{8}$ in. thick. Apart from the necessity for finishing the edges of plywood neatly, without glueing on a strip of veneer, which is troublesome but not difficult, this material is more suitable as it is not liable to warp or twist. The three parts of the top are hinged together using back flap hinges, but they must be let into the wood sufficiently deep to allow for the thickness of the knuckle.

The particular form of revolving hinge is shown as a separate detail. It should be fixed in the exact centre of the top and framing. Clean up the surfaces very carefully, using scraper and glasspaper, and apply wax polish rubbed in with a hard brush and polished with a soft cloth.

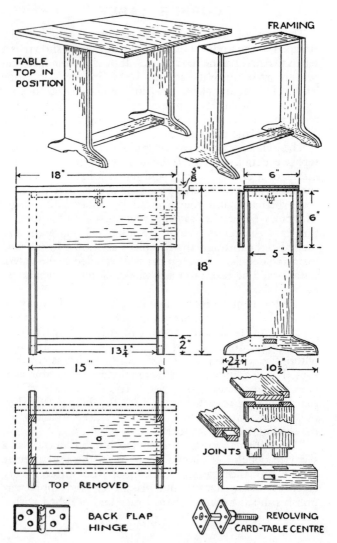

TABLE
TOP IN
POSITION

FRAMING

18"

⅛"

18"

6"

6"

5"

2"

13¼"

2¼"

10½"

15"

TOP REMOVED

JOINTS

BACK FLAP
HINGE

REVOLVING
CARD-TABLE CENTRE

145

TEA WAGON

This is a particularly useful piece of furniture, it contains nothing difficult in its construction, and can be made from wood machine-planed to width and thickness.

Birch is an excellent wood to use for the purpose. The most suitable soft wood is American whitewood, it is easier to work than birch and is suitable for stain or paint.

For the legs provide four 27 in. lengths of $1\frac{1}{4}$ in. by $1\frac{1}{4}$ in. wood finished size. The four long rails are 22 in. by $1\frac{1}{4}$ in. by $\frac{5}{8}$ in., and the short or end rails are 15 in. by $1\frac{1}{4}$ in. by $\frac{5}{8}$ in. The trays are of $\frac{1}{4}$ in. plywood measuring 22 in. by 15 in.

The rails are tenoned into the legs as shown in the enlarged separate details. Mark off the distance between the shoulders, $19\frac{1}{2}$ in. and $12\frac{1}{2}$ in. respectively. Set the marking gauge to $\frac{3}{8}$ in. and gauge lines from the face side of each piece. It will be seen that the top tenons are narrower, 1 in. instead of $1\frac{1}{4}$ in., this is because of the closeness of the tenon to the end of the wood.

Set out the positions of the mortises on the two inner edges of the legs as shown in the separate detail at the bottom of the page. The top mortise is $\frac{3}{4}$ in. down from a waste line about $\frac{1}{4}$ in. down. The lower mortise is $10\frac{3}{4}$ in. up from the bottom line, measured 26 in. below the top line. Check distance $12\frac{3}{4}$ in. between the two mortises.

Cut the mortises halfway through the wood, using a chisel measuring $\frac{3}{8}$ in. wide. Now saw the tenons, making quite sure that the thickness of mortise and tenon corresponds. The tops of rails can be rounded, and the top of legs chamfered. Glue up the joints, and then cut out $1\frac{1}{4}$ in. notches at the corners of the plywood trays. Fit in position and screw to the under edges of rails. Clean up with glasspaper. Bore holes for the special casters, stain or paint, and finally drive in the spring socket and the castor.

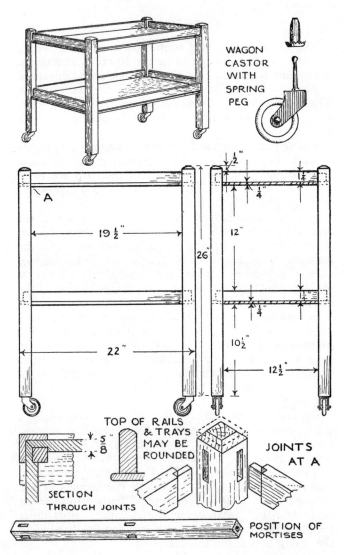

WAGON CASTOR WITH SPRING PEG

A

19½"

26"

22"

½"

¼"

12"

¼"

¼"

10½"

12½"

TOP OF RAILS & TRAYS MAY BE ROUNDED

⅝"

SECTION THROUGH JOINTS

JOINTS AT A

POSITION OF MORTISES

OAK CHEST

An oak chest is an interesting piece of constructional work for the handyman, especially if the surface is decorated with simple gouge cut carving. The design at Fig. 1 is adapted from an antique chest; the solid corners as at Fig. 2 simplify the construction. All dimensions are given in the portion of the front view (Fig. 3) and the side view (Fig. 4).

Prepare the four legs to the finished size, 1 ft. 8⅛ in. by 2 in. by 2 in., and from prepared lengths of 2 in. by ¾ in. wood cut off four long rails, 33 in., four end rails 14 in. and four intermediate uprights 16 in. long.

It will be seen in the plan at Fig. 5 that the rails are flush with the outside of the legs and that the panels on the sides and ends are fitted into grooves; those on the legs at A and on the rails should be made with a plough, although they can be cut with a chisel but it is a long job. The shoulders of the long rails are 30 in. apart, those of the short rails 11 in. and the uprights 13 in. The joints for the top and bottom rails are shown at B and C, and those of the uprights at D. With care in marking out and cutting to size, there should be no difficulty in jointing up the framework.

The bottom of the chest does not exactly conform to the original, but it is quite effective, being one piece of plywood ⅜ in. thick. It is fitted in grooves cut in the bottom rails as shown in the section at E (Fig. 5).

The lid of the chest is framed up with 2 in. by ⅞ in. wood as shown in half plan and section at Fig. 6. The panels in the lid are ⅝ in. thick, the sides are bevelled so that the top surface is on the same level as the framing. Hinge the lid with brass butts.

The photograph on page 159 shows the possibilities for decoration with simple thumb-cuts and knife or chisel cuts. Suggestions are given on pages 151 and 153 for suitable cuts.

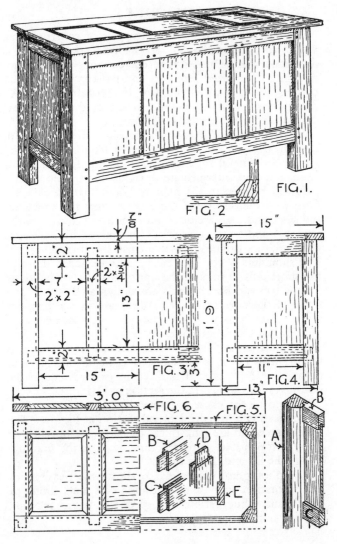

FIG. I.

FIG. 2

FIG. 3

FIG. 4

FIG. 5.

← FIG. 6.

7/8"

2"

7"

2' x 2'

2' x 3/4"

13"

15"

3"

1' 6"

15"

11"

13"

3' 0"

B

D

C

E

A

B

DECORATIVE CHISEL CUTS

There are considerable possibilities for decorative work in wood by using the chisel only, as shown in the next page. The first eight examples show simple treatments of the edge. The flat and hollow chamfers (1 and 2) are straightforward; in the case of long chamfers, a spokeshave can be used instead of a chisel. The short stopped chamfer (3) can be used in various ways, especially when combined with the corner cuts shown at 4. The three examples (5, 6 and 7) are simple variations of the previous cuts, they are suitable for straight and curved edges and also are easily curved out with a knife, but the cuts at 8 are more difficult but most effective. The example at 9 is worked by making vertical and sloping chisel cuts between two gauge lines, that at 10 is made by sloping cuts in opposite directions. Carefully spaced pencil lines should be drawn with a try-square.

A pleasing decorative cut is that shown at 11, the small squares are recessed to a depth of $\frac{1}{8}$ in. or so, the sides being quite vertical. A variation of the sloping cut is shown at 12; in order to obtain clean cuts the chisel should be the right width and must be ground to a thin angle and kept quite sharp.

The cuts shown at 13 and 14 form a most effective border decoration, especially for rails of small stools and similar constructional work. The angle of the cut should be about 90° and in small work the depth not more than $\frac{1}{8}$ in. First make clean vertical cuts, and then slice out the waste with the sharpest possible chisel.

The cuts shown at 15, 16 and 17, are those used by the chip carver and are quite simple. The pattern shown at 18 is formed by making vertical cuts to a depth of not more than $\frac{1}{8}$ in. and removing the waste between. The bottom of the recesses should be punched.

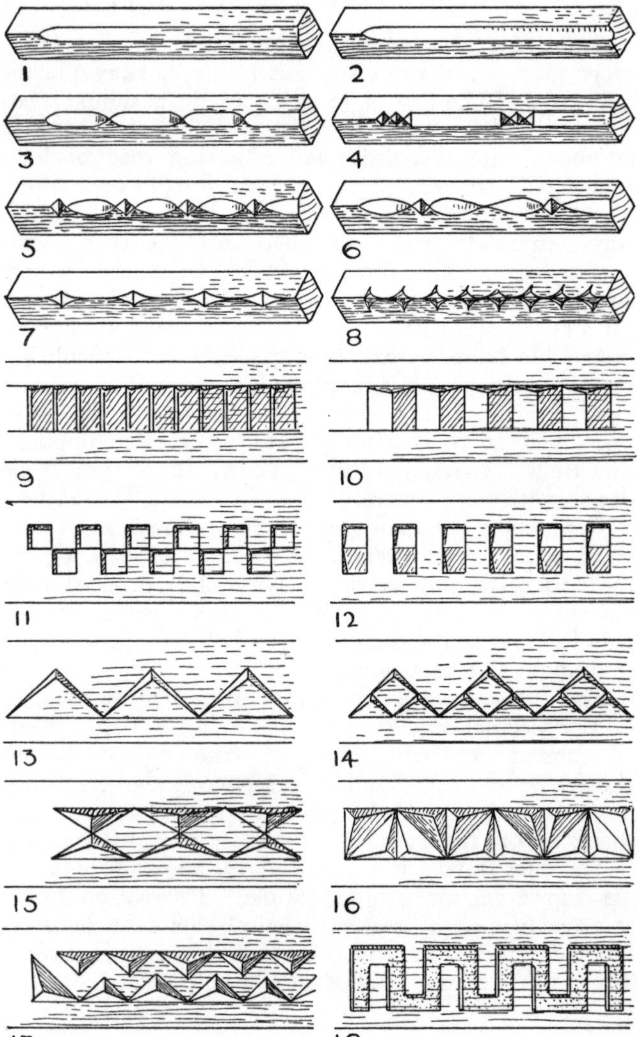
1
2
3
4
5
6
7
8
9
10
11
12
13
14
15
16
17
18

DECORATIVE GOUGE CUTS

Simple cuts, known as thumb cuts, made with a firmer gouge, form the basis of much decorative work in medieval woodwork. As a means of giving relief to plain surfaces it is still a most effective method of decoration. The examples at 1 and 2 are variations of the same cut. The long and round cuts at 3 form a pleasing decoration if they are done carefully, but in common with all similar gouge cuts, it is essential that the gouge should be kept perfectly sharp and under complete control. The gouge must be held firmly in one hand, with the fingers of the other acting as a guide. It is not advisable to attempt to reach the correct depth in one cut. Work down to it gradually. As a rule work against the running fibres in cuts with the grain. The pattern at 4 requires vertical cuts instead of the round cuts used at 3. The example at 5 combined the two cuts, 6 is a variation of 3 and 4.

The pattern at 7 is effective only when it is skilfully done, as also the more difficult parallel rows of long cuts at 8. These patterns should not be attempted without previous experience in the use of the gouge.

Practice in making simple gouge cuts will make it possible to carry out the traditional leaf form at 9, the centre and outside cuts are made first and then the sloping cuts are carefully spaced and cut. The pattern shown at 10 is a variation of the leaf form at 9; it makes an excellent border pattern. It will be seen that the patterns at 11 and 12 are but variations of the cuts used at 9. The suggestions given above are only a few of the possibilities for decorative work with a gouge. The examples to be seen on old chests will provide for much interesting work, adaptions can be arranged to suit individual taste.

The photographs on page 159 show a number of thumb and other gouge cuts.

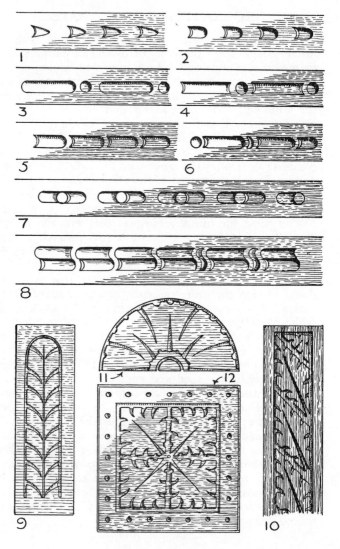

A BEDSIDE TABLE

At the top of the next page are two views of a useful bedside table. The upper portion consists of a table with a recess underneath. Immediately under the table is a hinged flap which is shown extended in the second view. The dimensions are given in the front and side views at the bottom of the page together with several constructional details.

With the exception of the door and under support, the material should be $\frac{1}{2}$ in. finished thickness, and the joints are tongued and grooved as shown at A, B and C. The two portions for the back are 36 in. high; one is 15 in. and the other $14\frac{1}{2}$ in. wide. The two shelves are $14\frac{3}{4}$ in. square, and are let into $\frac{1}{2}$ in. by $\frac{1}{4}$ in. grooves cut in the uprights; the top groove is 3 in. down and the other is 11 in. below. The side of the cupboard is $19\frac{1}{4}$ in. by $14\frac{1}{2}$ in., it is tongued to fit into a groove made in the shelf. The bottom of the cupboard is $14\frac{3}{4}$ in. by $14\frac{3}{4}$ in. and, as indicated at A, is tongued on both sides. A shelf should be fitted in grooves cut at a height of 11 in. inside the cupboard.

The joints at this stage should be glued together to form the main carcase. The door framing made of $1\frac{1}{2}$ in. by $\frac{3}{4}$ in. wood is mortised and tenoned at the corners in the usual way with provision for a $\frac{1}{4}$ in. thick plywood panel. The outside dimensions of the door are $18\frac{1}{2}$ in. by 14 in. The hinged flap is cut to $14\frac{1}{2}$ in. square, and the two corner brackets, one shown separately, has a length of 14 in., the other $14\frac{1}{2}$ in., both being $10\frac{1}{2}$ in. wide.

Screw the brackets together end to end, and then screw them to the flap, finally fix a hinge to the bracket and attach it to the upright as indicated.

Provide a handle and a ball catch for the door and finish with stain and polish, this should be done before the extending table and door are finally hinged in position.

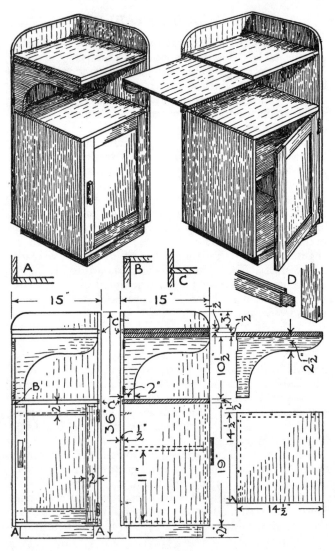

A   B   C   D

15″   15″   ⅛
3″
½
10½″
2″   2½″
C
B   36″   C   ½
½″
19   14½″
1″
2
A   A   2   14½″

CORNER WARDROBE

When space in the bedroom is limited, the design for a corner wardrobe, shown on the next page, will be found convenient. The main dimensions are given in the front and side views and a sectional plan at Figs. 1, 2 and 3. The back of the wardrobe is made up as two separate frames. For the frames, prepare three uprights 5 ft. 11¾ in. by 2½ in. by ⅞ in., and one similar in length and thickness but 2⅞ in. wide; also prepare four rails for top and bottom each 1 ft. 10 in. by 3 in. by ⅞ in., and two intermediate rails 1 ft. 10 in. by 4 in. by ⅞ in. Join with mortise and tenon joints and groove for ¼ in. plywood panels.

The side pieces, rebated to take the edges of the back pieces, are 5 ft. 11¼ in. by 6¾ in. by 1¼ in., the inside edges are planed to a mitre angle as shown in the detailed sketch at Fig. 4. The wider stile on one of the back pieces is rebated to form the back corner as shown at Fig. 5. The bottom board should be grooved into the lower rails of the back and front piece as shown in the details at Fig. 6 and 7. The top of the wardrobe is framed up with 3 in. by ¾ in. wood and covered with plywood fitted in a rebate cut in the framing as shown at Fig. 8. The front edges of the framing should be rounded to form a simple moulding.

The stiles of the doors are prepared to 5 ft. 5¾ in. long, those on the outside are 2½ in. wide and the other is 2¾ in. wide, all of them being ⅞ in. thick. The rails at the top are 3½ in. wide, those at the bottom are 5 in. wide, the inner rails being 4 in. wide. The joints and panelling are shown at Fig. 9 and the method of rebating the meeting stiles at Fig. 10. Hang the doors with butt hinges after accurate fitting.

Although the wardrobe can be made in oak, it is suitable for deal, finished with paint and combed in the way illustrated in the frontispiece.

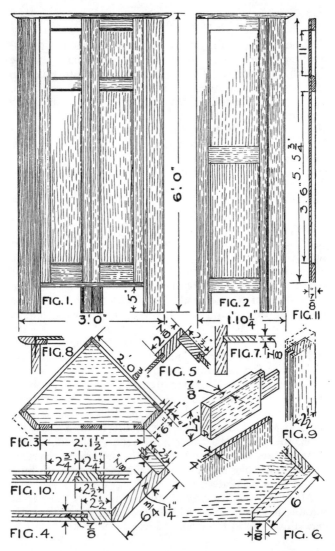

FIG. 1.

FIG. 2.

FIG 11

6' 0"

5"

3' 0"

1.10¼"

11"

3' 6". 5. 5¾"

⅞"

FIG. 8.

2' 0"

2⅜"

2½"

FIG. 5.

FIG. 7.

⅛

FIG. 3

2' 1½"

⅞

7/8

6"

2½"

2½"

4

FIG. 9.

2½

FIG. 10.

2¾"

2¼"

2½"

7/8

FIG. 4.

2½

7/8"

6¾ 1¼"

6"

⅞

FIG. 6.

157

WOOD FINISHING

The final preparation of the surface is just as important whether the wood has to be stained, polished or painted. However sharp the plane is, it is impossible to obtain a perfectly true surface. It is generally advisable to use a scraper to remove even the slightest ridges left by a plane. The ordinary flat steel scraper, used in a forward direction, is difficult to handle and to sharpen, but those of the hook variety shown in page 160, known as Skarsten, are simple and effective. A hook scraper is drawn in the direction of the grain and is easy to use.

Glasspaper should be applied with a block, and it should be noted that the best results are also obtained when the rubbing is parallel with and not across the grain.

Cellulose finish has the advantage of fairly rapid drying and ease of application for it leaves no brush marks. It is obtainable in small quantities in a wide range of colours as well as being available in comparatively transparent form.

Before the cellulose is applied, the surface after glasspapering should be filled with a plaster filler rubbed down with used glasspaper, or it may be coated with thin glue size. In the latter case it is advisable to apply two coats of size, both in turn, when quite dry, being lightly rubbed down with used glasspaper.

Two coats of cellulose are advisable, the first one being rubbed down when quite hard with pumice powder applied lightly with a felt pad. The painting should be done with a rubber-set brush of good quality, cheap articles sold as enamel brushes, are troublesome as the fibres fall out and may remain unnoticed until the paint is dry when they cannot be removed. Always avoid a draught when painting, it causes the paint to dry unevenly and is liable to deposit dust before the surface is dry.

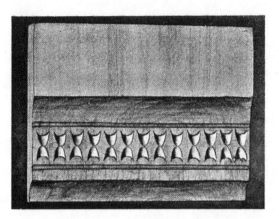

AN EFFECTIVE BORDER OF THUMBCUTS.

DECORATION WITH THUMBCUTS, GOUGE AND
CHISEL.

FRENCH POLISHING.

USING A HOOK SCRAPER.

USING GLASSPAPER. MAKE THE BLOCK WITH
WOOD COVERED WITH CORK.

FRENCH POLISHING

Although shellac varnish and cellulose have, in a large measure, taken the place of french polishing, the latter is still a highly satisfactory way of obtaining a hard lasting polish.

With either method it is essential that the surface of the wood should be properly prepared. After the wood has been planed smooth and true, the surface should be rubbed over with glasspaper, which should be wrapped over a block of wood. For flat surfaces, the block should be as large as possible, 5 in. by $3\frac{1}{2}$ in. is a convenient size. For mouldings small rounds of wood can be utilised.

Before polishing it is also necessary to "fill" the grain or pores of wood with a suitable medium. Prepared wood fillers are sold, but ordinary plaster of paris, moistened with water and rubbed into the pores with a piece of rag, makes an excellent filler. Clean off with fine glasspaper moistened with oil to remove the "bite."

The process of polishing consists of applying shellac dissolved in methylated spirits with a pad or rubber. The pad is of cotton wool enclosed in a linen rag. The polish is allowed to soak into the cotton wool before it is covered with the rag, the latter being twisted at the top to form a pear-shaped pad. Hold the pad with the large portion at the back and then proceed with the rubbing. Do not work with anything but a firm circular movement, and add a little more polish from time to time. When a sufficient body of polish is formed, add a little spirit to a small quantity of polish and continue, gradually increasing the proportion of spirit in order to harden the surface. The final process is to dust the surface with prepared chalk and rub lightly with a fine linen pad.

The photographs on page 160 illustrate the methods of using a scraper and of French polishing.

GARDEN PATHS AND EDGING IN CONCRETE

In preparing for a concrete path it is necessary to have a sound foundation and good drainage ; the soil, should therefore be removed for a depth of at least 9 in. The excavated portion is built up to within 3 in. of the required height with broken bricks and stones and thoroughly well rammed.

Prepare some side strips of wood, about 21 in. by 1 in., with stakes as indicated at Fig. 1. Care should be taken to fix these border pieces level and parallel. The concrete is mixed according to the instructions on page 164, and spread evenly between the strips of wood. Level the concrete by means of a strip of wood as shown, drawn backwards and forwards until the surface is level. If a rounded surface or camber is desired, use a hollow rod as at Fig. 2. As it may not be possible to complete the whole of the path with one mixing of concrete, one section should be completed before the next lot of concrete is laid down, in this case fit a bar across the path to keep the concrete from spreading, remove it before the next section is laid.

Path edging similar in section to that shown at Fig. 3 is easily made in a mould made of $\frac{3}{4}$ in. or 1 in. wood as at Fig. 4. The bottom corners of the mould, instead of being square are filled in with Scotia moulding as indicated at Fig. 5, this forms the corner shape.

Three-cornered wood in the corners of the mould will give a section as at Fig. 6. Edging tiles as at Fig. 7 may be made in a flat open mould as shown at Fig. 8. The curved blocks at Fig. 9 give a rounded top and triangular pieces (Fig. 10) make the lower example. Slabs for a crazy path as shown at Fig. 11 can be made similarly to a larger scale by using a mould shaped in the way illustrated at Fig. 12. In all cases, the mould should be wetted before the concrete mixture is poured in.

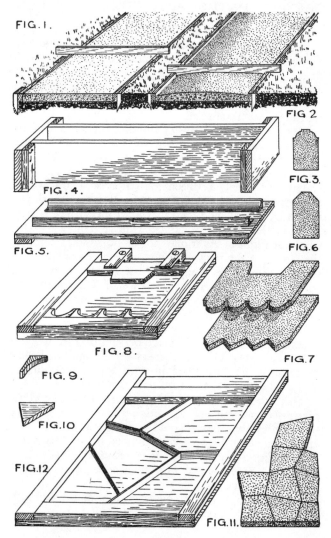

FIG. 1.

FIG 2

FIG. 3.

FIG. 4.

FIG. 5.

FIG. 6

FIG. 8.

FIG. 7

FIG. 9.

FIG. 10

FIG. 12

FIG. 11.

163

MIXING CONCRETE

Concrete is made by mixing Portland cement, sand and gravel in varying proportions, with sufficient water to bind them together. For all general purposes the proportions are 1 : 2 and 4.

Portland cement can be obtained in bags of 7 lbs. and upwards, and should be kept in a dry place until used. Sand graded for the purpose as well as gravel, otherwise known as aggregate, is sold by the cubic yard. Instead of gravel, the aggregate may be composed of broken stone, marble or granite chippings. The aggregate should be clean and free from dirt and dust.

An estimate of the quantity of material required should be made before the work is begun. For example, if it is required to make a concrete path 36 ft. long, 3 ft. wide and 3 in. deep, this works out in the proportion of 1, 2 and 4, as follows, $\frac{1}{4} \times \frac{3}{1} \times \frac{36}{1} = 27$ cu. ft. or 1 cu. yd.; this quantity of concrete uses 5 cwt. of cement, $4\frac{1}{2}$ cu. ft. sand and 9 cu. ft. of aggregate. With these figures it will be possible to make the required calculations for any quantity of concrete. It is advisable to make a wooden measure so that the quantities can be mixed accurately.

To prepare the material spread the aggregate on a large board, or on a hard path, and cover with the sand. Mix together with a spade and then add the cement, and mix again thoroughly. Pour the water from a water-can through a rose and mix again. The concrete should not be too wet, but just wet enough to move off the spade.

Considerable care should be taken with the mixing to make quite sure that all the ingredients are incorporated.

Always place the concrete in position immediately after it is made. In order to prevent waste only just the quantity required should be mixed at one time, for mixed concrete that has partly dried cannot be restored by adding water.

CONCRETE PLANT POTS.

CONCRETE BIRD BATH AND SEAT.

COLOURED CONCRETE

In positions where the plain grey of ordinary concrete is not suitable and for various ornamental purposes, it is possible to colour the cement before it is mixed with the sand and aggregate. Cement already coloured in two or three shades can be purchased ready for use, but it is a simple matter to add a colouring pigment to finely ground cement and so obtain distinctive colourings.

RED. 85 parts cement, 15 parts red oxide of iron (ferric oxide).

PINK. 97 parts cement, 3 parts crimson lake (alumina base).

YELLOW. 88 parts cement, 12 parts yellow ochre.

BLUE. 85 parts cement, 15 parts azure blue.

GREEN. 90 parts cement, 10 parts oxide of chromium.

BROWN. 88 parts cement, 6 parts black oxide of manganese, 4 parts red oxide of iron, 2 parts black oxide of iron or copper.

BLACK. 90 parts cement, 10 parts of any carbon black.

WHITE. 67 parts cement, 33 parts powdered chalk.

In all cases it is essential that the colouring matter should be mixed most thoroughly with the cement before it is mixed with the sand and aggregate.

Another method of obtaining a coloured effect is to use a richly coloured aggregate. Granite chippings, red sandstone, richly coloured gravel, marble chippings are all suitable. Mix with the cement and sand in the usual way. It is also possible to use broken coloured glass, the finer the better. Concrete made in this way has considerable decorative possibilities. It can be used for making garden pots as well as for walls, paths, etc. Before the concrete has set really hard expose the aggregate by rubbing the surface with a stiff brush, a wire brush is suitable. This has the effect of removing the film of cement and will bring out the colour of the aggregate.

PLANT POTS IN CONCRETE

The diagrams on the next page show how to make the mould for the plant pot shown on page 165. First of all decide on the inside dimensions, these will determine the size of the core shown at Fig. 1. This core should be made of $\frac{3}{4}$ in. wood in the form of a box. The three round rods projecting on the top of the core form drainage holes in the finished pot.

The base is shown at Fig. 2, it is made of $\frac{3}{4}$ in. or 1 in. thick wood. The size of the base should allow for the thickness of the sides of the pot, of the outside boards and the blocks required to support the boards. The side and end boards are shown at Fig. 3 and 4; these should be at least $\frac{3}{4}$ in. thick and the end pieces should fit between the side pieces. Supposing the core measures 15 in. by 9 in. by 5 in. and the thickness of the pot is $1\frac{1}{2}$ in., the side pieces should measure, providing the board used is $\frac{3}{4}$ in. thick, $19\frac{1}{2}$ in. by $7\frac{1}{2}$ in. The end pieces for the same mould would be 12 in. by $7\frac{1}{2}$ in.

The slabs of wood shown at Figs. 3 and 4 should be not more than $\frac{1}{4}$ in. thick. They are nailed on and the nail holes filled with putty, plastic wood or cement. Any marks left on the exposed surface of the mould will be reproduced on the cement. In order to obtain a smooth surface on the outside of the pot, it is necessary to have smooth surfaces on the mould. The two end battens on the base should be 2 in. wide and 1 in. thick, those at the sides need not be more than $1\frac{1}{2}$ in. wide. For the pot in question the base should measure 25 in. by $16\frac{1}{2}$ in. approximately. To complete the mould make two clamps to fit on the ends as shown at Fig. 5. From the above description, the mould for the other pot shown on page 165 will not be difficult to make. A 1, 2 and 4 mixture of concrete should be used, and the mould wetted with water before the concrete is poured in.

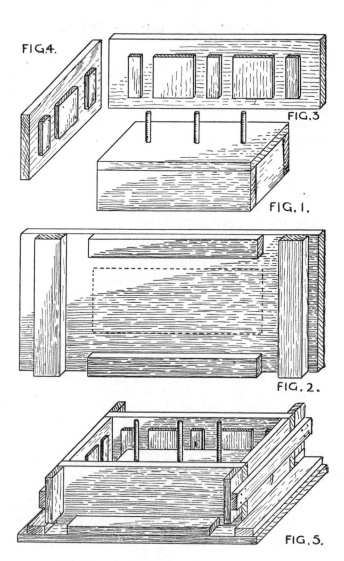

FIG.4.

FIG.3

FIG. 1.

FIG. 2.

FIG. 5.

CONCRETE GARDEN SEAT

The seat shown at the bottom of the page 166 is an example of reinforced concrete and it requires two moulds made as shown on the next page.

The frame at Fig. 1 is made to the length, width and thickness of the seat, the latter should be from $2\frac{1}{2}$ in. to 3 in. This frame is not joined at the corners in any way, but rests on a base board and is supported on brackets nailed on as at Fig. 2. The base board need not be more than $\frac{3}{4}$ in. thick, but it should be stiffened by battens nailed on underneath. The oblong slabs shown inside should be the same size as the width and thickness of the legs and about 1 in. thick; they form recesses for the legs to fit into. The method of forming the decorative recesses on the front edge of the seat is shown at Fig. 4, half round wood as at Fig. 5 being used.

The re-inforcement is provided by lengths of stout iron wire or thin rod, as shown at Fig. 3, by a piece of expanded metal, or even stout wire netting, attached by string to two or more rods across the top and placed about half way down the mould.

The mould for the legs is shown at Fig. 6. In this case there is no need for re-inforcement as they should be about 4 in. thick. The same base can be used, the sides of the frame being made wider and the length reduced by a cross piece as indicated at Fig. 7. The blocks on the end of the cross piece, 1 in. thick, and the space between corresponds with the recesses allowed for the seat mould. The decoration on the front of the legs is formed by half-round pieces secured to the side of the mould as shown at Fig. 8. Care should be taken in nailing on the strips to avoid bruising the half round lengths. Nail holes should be filled up and all surfaces left smooth. A 1, 2 and 4 concrete mixture is suitable for the seat.

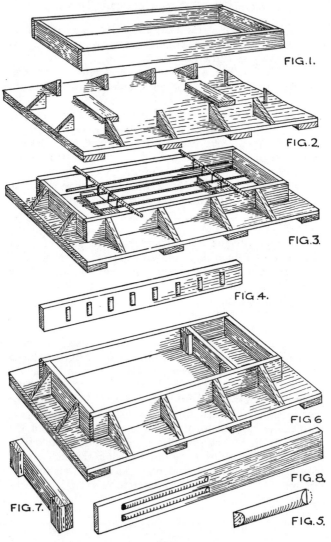

FIG.I.

FIG.2.

FIG.3.

FIG.4.

FIG 6

FIG.7.

FIG.8.

FIG.5.

BIRD BATH

A particularly attractive design for a bird bath is shown on page 166. It is not difficult to cast, but the moulds are somewhat troublesome to make. The principal dimensions for the bath are given in a section, Fig. 1 on the next page and from these sizes the necessary moulds can be made.

The bath itself is octagonal in plan with a diameter of 24 in. and a thickness of 2½ in. The base board should be at least 3 ft. square, made of ¾ in. wood nailed down to battens of 2 in. by 1 in. Mark out the octagon on the board and then fit the sides, using 2½ in. by ¾ in. wood with ¼ in. thick projections, nailed on as shown. The side pieces are supported by stout blocks of wood nailed to the board. The recess in the bath is formed by triangular strips fitted on as shown at Fig. 3, the height should not amount to more than 1¼ in. The recesses for the legs should be provided by 2½ in. by 2½ in. by 1 in. blocks nailed to the underside of strips fastened to the top of the mould. Care must be taken to fix them in the correct position, and to finish all the joints neatly, any defect in the mould will show on the finished work. This applies particularly to nail holes.

The same base board can be used for the legs, the shape being marked out accurately. First enclose the outside lines with a framework, this will give a space of 22 in. by 10¾ in. The shape should be built up by various strips of wood as indicated at Fig. 4. Each part should be dealt with in turn in relation to the actual dimensions. The bottom slab is quite a simple job, the mould is octagonal, the height of the sides being 2½ in. The recesses for the legs are formed by two blocks, 8½ in. by 2½ in. by 2½ in., halved together in the middle and screwed to the centre of the mould. Support on a concrete foundation.

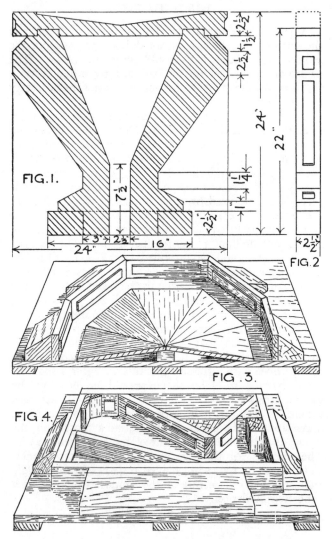

FIG.1.

FIG.2

FIG.3.

FIG.4.

$7\frac{1}{2}''$

$2\frac{1}{2}''$

$2\frac{1}{2}''$ $1\frac{1}{2}''$ $2\frac{1}{2}''$

24"

22"

$2\frac{1}{2}''$

$1\frac{1}{4}''$

1"

3" $2\frac{1}{2}''$

24"

16"

BRICKWORK FOUNDATIONS

Bricklaying is quite within the capacity of the handyman and for the erection of pillars for a pergola as illustrated on page 201, for a garden wall or for the erection of a workshop, the work will be found quite straightforward.

On the opposite page is shown six layers of brickwork for a pier or pillar, beginning with the foundation layer or footing, using plain bricks and ordinary mortar. Before the bricks are laid it will be necessary to prepare a solid and level foundation of concrete. The thickness of the concrete will depend on the weight of the brickwork to be placed upon it. For the purpose of a pillar to support a pergola it will be sufficient to have a 4 in. layer of concrete, but on very firm ground this may be reduced to 2 in. if the three footing courses indicated are laid on the concrete.

An ordinary 1, 2 and 4 mixture of concrete should be used, and for purposes of economy all the foundation holes should be filled with concrete at the one mixing.

Good mortar is essential in bricklaying, and for ordinary purposes a lime mortar will be found suitable; this is composed of one part of slated lime and three parts of sand. These materials can be obtained from a builder ready to mix to the required consistency with water. It may be found more convenient to use a cement mortar, 4 parts of sand to one of cement. It is certainly advisable for the footings. The mortar should be laid to a thickness of about $\frac{1}{2}$ in. and the bricks pressed into it with the handle of the trowel, the actual joint being no more than $\frac{1}{4}$ in. at the most. When the mortar has been pressed out clean the mortar away from the joints with a trowel as the work proceeds. The drawings on the next page show the way in which the bricks should be laid. A level and a plumb line will be required as the work progresses.

BUILDING A BRICK WALL

The three sketches on the previous page show the method of placing the bricks in building a 9 in. wall in English bond. The two general methods, English and Flemish, of laying bricks for the walls of a house allow for bonding; in the present case the bonding is carried out by placing one row of bricks lengthwise as " stretchers " and the next row sideways or " headers."

The first row of bricks, known as the footings, are laid on a concrete foundation, they consist of bricks placed in the positions shown in the top drawing, but it would be better to use " closers " to break the joints. It should be noted that a solid foundation of concrete is essential, and its depth depends on the height of the wall. For a low wall of 10 courses the foundation need not be more than 4 in. deep. If the wall is higher, about 6 to 9 in. of concrete will be needed, depending on the nature of the subsoil. The concrete should be a 1, 2 and 4 mixture, and it should be trued up with a level placed on a straight batten of wood.

The position of the wall must be marked off with a line, and it is advisable to build up the two ends of the wall so that a line can be stretched from one end to the other; this will enable the bricks to be laid level and in line. It will be noticed that the hollow portion of the brick is uppermost.

As it is important to keep the wall upright, a plumb line hung on a board should be used frequently. Each brick as it is laid should be tapped down with the handle of the trowel, and the joints pointed with the edge of the trowel as the work progresses. It will be seen that in order to retain the bonding, a " closer " or half-width brick is placed at the end of the " header " courses.

Cement mortar in the proportion of 3 or 4 to 1 should be used for the footings and may be used entirely in building the wall.

GARDEN ROLLER IN CONCRETE

The concrete roller shown at Fig. 1 will be found quite as serviceable as a more expensive iron roller. The size will depend on individual requirements, but as it is possible to obtain the necessary mould in the form of an empty oil drum, the variations in size of these receptacles will provide a choice. Failing an oil drum, two circular pieces of wood can be prepared and ordinary tinned sheet nailed on the circumference. Holes should be left so that the concrete can be poured inside.

The drum must be centred very carefully at both ends, and some trouble should be taken to find the exact centre. Provide a length of gas barrel for the axle, 1 in. diameter will not be too large. Find a drill of the same diameter as the pipe, drill holes at each end, and insert the pipe which should be cut off about 2 in. beyond the ends of the drum. In the event of the top of the drum being damaged, thus rendering it impossible to make a centre hole, a strip of wood may be secured across the top as at Fig. 2, and the axle fixed in it.

It is presumed that the drum will be empty and contain no rubbish, oil on the sides does not matter. Holes must be cut in the top at one end so that the concrete mixture can be poured inside. Use a stick in order to tamp down the concrete, and be careful when filled that the surface is neatly levelled off. After the concrete has set the case can be left on if desired, but a neater job results when it is removed.

The suggestion for a handle for a medium sized roller, given at Fig. 3, can be made from 1 in. by $\frac{1}{4}$ in. iron bar, any blacksmith will make it for a small charge; a wooden handle as at Fig. 4 can be bolted on. Another method of providing the handle is shown at Fig. 5, this is made of readily procured gas pipe fittings as at Fig. 6.

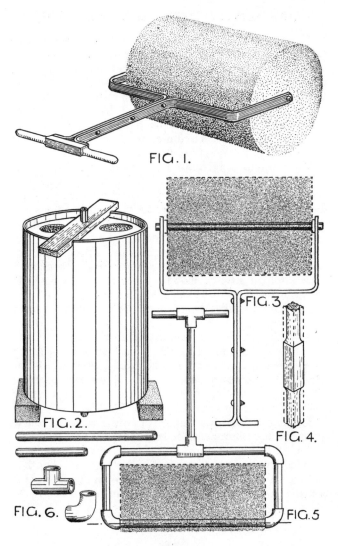

FIG. I.

FIG. 2.

FIG. 3.

FIG. 4.

FIG. 5.

FIG. 6.

CLEANING THE SEWING MACHINE

A sewing machine should, as far as possible, be kept free from dust, but it is impossible to prevent particles of dust and fluff finding their way into the working parts. In time, if cleaning is neglected, the accumulation of the dust will tend to interfere with the freedom of the running parts. Another cause of trouble is the use of inferior and unsuitable oil. Only the special oil supplied by the makers of the machine, or a fine machine oil such as 3 in 1, should be used. Failing a supply of the correct lubricant, paraffin can be used as a temporary measure, but not as a rule.

In dealing with a machine normally kept under cover when not in use, it will be found that a soft camel hair brush dipped in paraffin can be used to collect up dust and fluff particles. Usually it will be sufficient to remove the face plate to clean the disc operating the needle bar and to clean all the exposed parts underneath the bed plate. The bevel gear or cranked spindle can be examined, but it is only in a much neglected machine that this will be necessary. To remove old and clogged oil from any of these parts, a wash with petrol will be sufficient.

It is important that all moving parts in contact must be covered with a film of oil and not allowed to become dry. Oil should always be applied at the points indicated in the diagram at Fig. 1, a drop of oil being sufficient at any place. It is a mistake to allow a flow of oil at any point, a drop frequently applied is better than a lot at once. The photograph at Fig. 2 shows some of the cleaning points.

In a Singer machine it is important that oil should be applied at the point marked A when the take-up lever is at its lowest point. After oiling run the machine for a few minutes so that the oil may penetrate into the bearings.

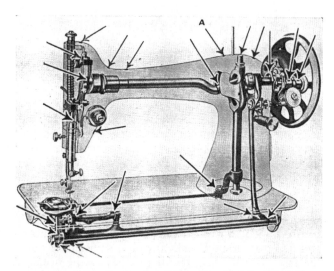

FIG. 1.   THE OILING POINTS OF A SINGER SEWING
MACHINE.

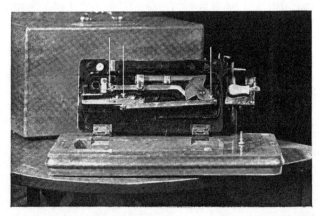

SHOWING PLACES WHERE DUST AND FLUFF COLLECTS.

OIL SHOULD BE APPLIED AT THE POSITIONS SHOWN.

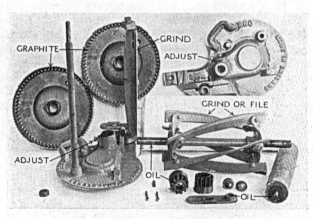

THE MOWER DISMANTLED FOR OVERHAULING,
CLEANING, PAINTING AND OILING.

OVERHAULING THE LAWN MOWER

In order to keep a lawn mower in good condition, it should be wiped dry and cleaned after use, unfortunately it is often neglected during the winter, rust is allowed to form and consequently does more damage than any amount of service. It is a good plan to keep a cheap paint brush handy for cleaning purposes after use and this, with an oily or vaseline rag, will at least prevent rust.

During the winter the mower should be taken apart so that each portion can be thoroughly cleaned and oiled and where necessary painted. Three parts of the mower call for special attention, the bearings, the cylinder and the fixed blade. The spindle of the cylinder should run easily in the bearings without play. If the bearings are worn they should be renewed. In the cheaper qualities of mower the plain sleeve bearings cannot be adjusted, but with better machines, ample opportunity is provided for adjustment and the bearings will last for many years before they need be renewed.

The rotating blades of the cylinder are liable to get bent and otherwise damaged by stones. They should be straightened out and tested ; a good plan is to support the spindle on a couple of grooved blocks and in rotating note any difference in the distance between the blade and the bench. If the blades are much out of truth, they should be ground by a professional, but with care they can be trued up with a flat file.

The fixed blade is also liable to damage by stones, but the grinding is a much simpler job, and care should be taken to retain the exact angle. The travelling wheels and driving pinions should be carefully cleaned, first with paraffin and then coated with graphite. When re-assembling, the rotating cutters should be adjusted so that they will cut newspaper.

SUN BLINDS

Two methods of making sun blinds are shown on the next page. The first one is made by attaching a spring roller to the top of the window frame. The roller should be a Hartshorn spring roller 1 in. diameter and long enough to reach from one side of the brickwork to the other, less the allowance for the blocks of wood necessary for the support of the front board required to protect the blind. The front of the hood should be shaped to fit inside the arch and be deep enough to cover the roller. Wood of at least $\frac{1}{2}$ in. thick should be used. The method of fixing the roller is by means of brackets, which can be screwed to the woodwork of the window frame. One end of the blind material is fastened to the roller, the other end to a hinged strut with allowance for a flap. The strut should be made of $\frac{1}{4}$ in. round iron rod, which should be bent to the shape shown and pivoted in wall plates secured to the brickwork with rawlplugs. A cord fastened to the strut should be secured to a cleat screwed to the bottom of the window.

The other form of blind is made of reeds. It is rolled up and down by means of a cord passing through a pully. In this case also the blind, when rolled up, should be protected by a hood or shield flush with the outside brickwork similar to that used for the spring blind.

The top of the blind is fastened directly to the top of the window frame, and behind it is one end of a long cord. An iron side pulley is screwed to the frame just above the top of the blind and the cord is threaded through and brought down to the sill where it can be fastened to a cleat. The blind, when dropped to the bottom of the window, should not be entirely unrolled, otherwise it will not roll up when the cord is pulled.

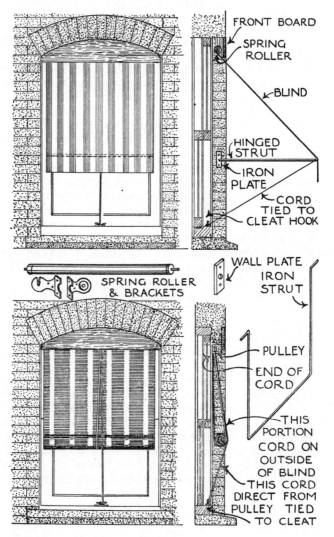

FRONT BOARD

SPRING ROLLER

BLIND

HINGED STRUT

IRON PLATE

CORD TIED TO CLEAT HOOK

SPRING ROLLER & BRACKETS

WALL PLATE IRON STRUT

PULLEY

END OF CORD

THIS PORTION CORD ON OUTSIDE OF BLIND THIS CORD DIRECT FROM PULLEY TIED TO CLEAT

CUPBOARD BEDSTEADS

A simple method of fitting a bedstead into a recess is shown on the next page. The framework in position is shown at Fig. 1. The cupboard is shown closed at Fig. 2. The width of spring mattress to be fitted on framework depends on the size of the recess or on individual requirements. Stock sizes of frames range from lengths of 6 ft. 3 in., and 5 ft. 11 in., with widths from 30 in. to 54 in. Mattresses can be obtained with coil springs ready to fit on the frame and secured by using iron clips to screw on the side of the wood frame.

Having decided on length and width, the wooden frame as shown at Fig. 3 should be made from $2\frac{1}{2}$ in. by $1\frac{1}{2}$ in. hard wood. The long sides should be about 3 in. longer than the mattress and the outside made to suit the actual width. When the dimensions of the frame have been decided, make it up with the two cross pieces, tenoned and pinned, as shown at Fig. 4. The sides of the recess are now packed up with suitable pieces of wood as shown at Fig. 3, in order to allow clearance.

The frame should be attached to the packing with two coach screws (Fig. 6) at a convenient height, and set back to allow for the thickness of the overlay mattress and bed clothes, and then a hinged support as shown at Fig. 5 should be fitted to the inside of the framing at the same height.

Suitable doors can be made with plywood stiffened with $1\frac{1}{2}$ in. by $\frac{1}{2}$ in. wood as shown at Figs. 7 and 8. The framing should be made with halving joints as shown at Fig. 9.

The door opening should be wide enough and high enough to clear the frame with an allowance of 2 in. or 3 in. for the overhanging bed clothes. By the means of a row of round-headed screws on the side of the frame, a cord can be laced from one side to the other to retain the clothes when the bed is placed in the recess.

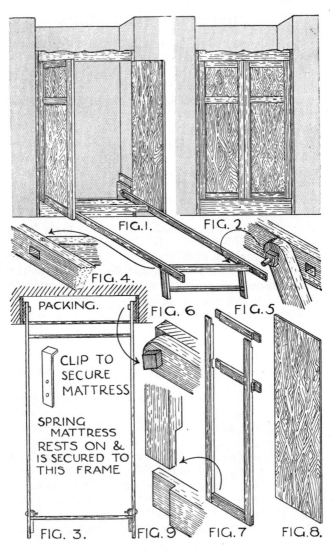

FIG.1.

FIG.2.

FIG. 4.

FIG. 5.

PACKING.

FIG. 6.

CLIP TO
SECURE
MATTRESS

SPRING
MATTRESS
RESTS ON &
IS SECURED TO
THIS FRAME

FIG. 3.

FIG. 9.

FIG. 7.

FIG. 8.

WALL TABLES

Details are given on the next page for three kinds of wall table. The simplest form, shown at Figs. 1, 2 and 3 consists of a wall plate to which are screwed two steel table-flap brackets. The table is hinged to a strip of similar thickness nailed to the top of the wall plate. The latter should be fixed to the wall with rawlplugs. The brackets are obtained in lengths from 6 in. to 16 in., this will determine the length and width of the table top.

A double-purpose wall table is shown at Figs. 4 and 5. The brackets supporting the table top are utilised as supports for rods intended to be used for airing. The table can be made to any convenient size, but the brackets should be wide enough, especially at the back, to give good support. The rods joining the two brackets can be $\frac{3}{4}$ in. dowelling, fitted in as shown in the detail at D. Hinge the table to a wide wall plate secured with rawlplugs, and fasten a button as at Fig. 5 to the wall by the same means. It will be seen that the airer may still be used when the table is in position. It should prove a useful addition to the conveniences of a kitchen.

The wall table shown in side view at Fig. 6 and in end view at Fig. 7 is useful for ironing. Suitable dimensions are given. Prepare a wall plate 18 in. by 3 in. by 1 in. with a top strip 18 in. by 2 in. by $\frac{3}{4}$ in. Fix with rawlplugs to the wall at a height of 30 in. ; prepare the top to 30 in. by 18 in., it will be found that $\frac{3}{4}$ in. plywood is ideal for the purpose. Cut out the leg to a length of $29\frac{1}{4}$ in. and 6 in. wide, taper to 2 in. and hinge under the front end. Prepare a spring clip to take 2 in., fix under table and then hinge the top to the wall plate with a pair of cross garnet hinges as shown. To close table, fold leg to catch in clip and allow to fall.

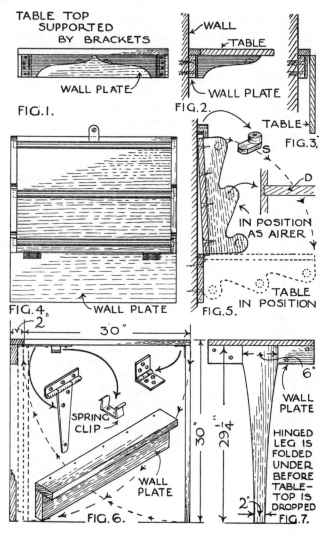

TABLE TOP
SUPPORTED
BY BRACKETS

WALL

TABLE

WALL PLATE

WALL

TABLE

WALL PLATE

FIG. 1.

FIG. 2.

TABLE

FIG. 3.

S

D

IN POSITION
AS AIRER

TABLE
IN POSITION

FIG. 4.

WALL PLATE

FIG. 5.

2"

30"

SPRING
CLIP

WALL
PLATE

30"

6"

WALL
PLATE

29¼"

HINGED
LEG IS
FOLDED
UNDER
BEFORE
TABLE-
TOP IS
DROPPED

2"

FIG. 6.

FIG. 7.

TRELLIS FOR THE GARDEN

The ordinary form of expanding trellis as shown at Fig. 1 is very inexpensive and when securely fixed to suitable supports and coated with a wood preservative it serves its purpose, but unless it is supported in a suitable manner it will not stand much strain. A more pleasing form of trellis is that shown at Fig. 2. This can be made quite easily from prepared strips similar to that used for making expanding trellis. In all forms of trellis it is advisable to finish with a capping as shown in section at Fig. 3. One disadvantage of grooved capping is that the trellis has to be bent and forced into the groove. A better way is to use narrow strips, as indicated at Fig. 4, nailed each side of the trellis and to nail a plain chamfered capping on top.

It is generally advisable to nail the bottom of the trellis to a fairly wide board as at Fig. 5, this has a valuable stiffening effect on the whole width, especially when supported by suitable posts at frequent intervals.

Pleasing patterns of square trellis for use as a decorative feature or in training various climbing plants are shown at Figs. 6 and 7. The uprights should be about 1½ in. by 1½ in. in section, and should be sunk in the ground at least 18 in. The horizontal members of the trellis can be fitted into mortises, or instead, the uprights can be grooved on the inside to receive them. Figs. 8 to 10 show methods of securing trellis to the top of walls and fences. The uprights need not be more than 1½ in. by 1½ in., but they should be secured very firmly to the walls or fence, rawlplugs should be used in the former case. Horizontal rails at the bottom and capping on the top as shown at Fig. 9 are advisable. In no case should the application of wood preservative be forgotten, and all portions of the wood fixed in the ground should be coated with tar or pitch.

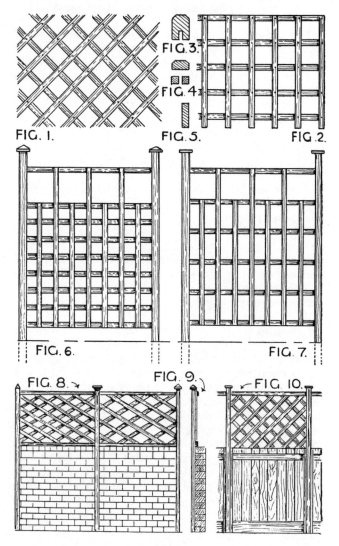

FIG. 1.

FIG. 3.

FIG. 4.

FIG. 5.

FIG. 2.

FIG. 6.

FIG. 7.

FIG. 8.

FIG. 9.

FIG 10.

LATH FENCING

The sketch at Fig. 1 shows a simple form of fencing inexpensive to make and quite durable. It is important that the upright supports should be sunk into the ground at intervals as indicated at Fig. 2, which shows a side view. The plan of the fence at Fig. 3 shows that the capping completely covers the interlacing of the laths.

The various parts of the fence are shown at Fig. 4. The uprights are spaced at regular intervals from 6 ft. to 8 ft. For a 3 ft. high fence the uprights should be 5 ft. by 2 in. by 1 in., with 2 ft. buried in the ground. For foot and struts, provide six 2 ft. lengths of the same material. The uprights at B should also be of 2 in. by 1 in. wood, but they need not be more than 3 ft. high.

The uprights at A should be nailed together with a 5 ft. by 1 in. by ½ in. between, two of the 2 ft. lengths should be nailed across the bottom, and the remaining four nailed on in the form of struts as shown at Fig. 2. The whole of the lower portion should be coated with tar or pitch. All the uprights required should be prepared together, and the groove cut for the skirtings of 6 in. by ½ in. boards, these are nailed on as shown at Fig. 5. When the necessary holes have been dug, the uprights should be placed in position and trued up before the holes are filled in.

The laths shown at L should be 2 in. by ½ in., and long enough to interlace and fit into the grooves left in the uprights. Two strips are nailed on each side at the top, and finally the capping at C should be nailed on. The fence shown at Fig. 6, with details at Fig. 7, is made similarly but the laths are those used by builders for ceilings, they are cheap, easily obtained, and form a sound fence. Owing to the small size of the laths and the short length, more care is needed in making the fence. Creosote or a prepared wood preservative should be used to finish the fence.

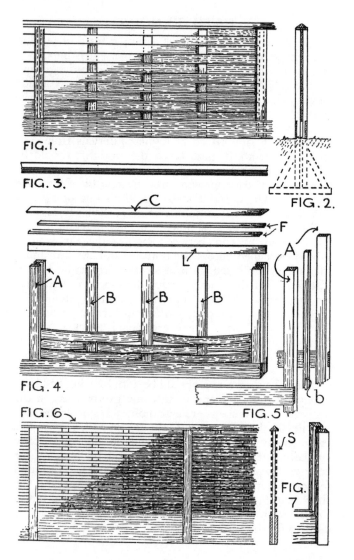

FIG. 1.

FIG. 3.

FIG. 2.

C

F

L

A

B   B   B

A

b

FIG. 4.

FIG. 5.

FIG. 6.

S

FIG. 7.

WOODEN FENCING

Detailed measurements of the ordinary type of wooden fence are given at Figs. 1 and 2. Built usually of oak it is simple in construction and it can be erected quickly. It will be seen that the main posts are let into the ground to a depth of 3 ft., this is not too deep if the fence is to stand the strain of strong winds. Oak suitable for fencing is generally to be obtained at any timber yard, but well seasoned timber should always be used. It is of great importance to prevent decay in the portion of the post below ground. One method is to char the outside surface, another is to coat it very thoroughly with pitch, tar or creosote ; the latter two preservatives being allowed to sink into the grain.

It will be seen at Fig. 3 that the boards of the fence fit close together, and in either painting or creosoting the touching edges should not be forgotten ; it is a good plan to paint each upright at least with one coat of the particular form of preservative used before it is nailed in position.

Open fences or railings are made as shown at Figs. 4 and 5, the dimensions may be varied slightly, but it will be found that the sizes given in the sketch will work out satisfactorily. With a low fence there is no need to let the posts into the ground more than 2 ft. 6 in.

The sketch of an open fence at Fig. 6 shows how the upright palings are spaced on the horizontal bars.

Split oak fences as shown at Fig. 7 are made in the same way as the other examples, the upright laths should overlap for at least 1 in. The material for filling in the framework is available in several widths. One of 4 in. will be found most useful. Oak fences should be protected by varnish ; when made of deal, the fence may be painted or coated with creosote or wood preservative. If paint is used, nothing less than three coats should be applied.

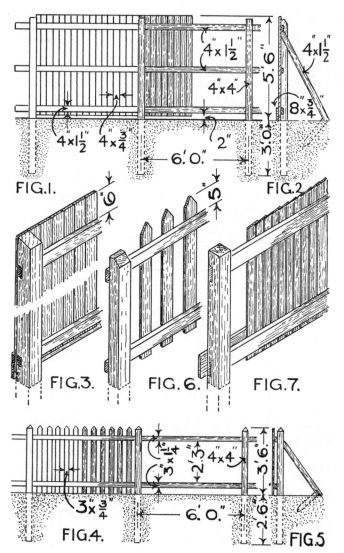

FIG.1.

$4'' \times 1\frac{1}{2}''$

$4'' \times 4''$

$4'' \times 1\frac{1}{2}''$

$4'' \times \frac{3}{4}''$

$8'' \times \frac{3}{4}''$

5'.6"

3'.0"

2"

6'. 0."

FIG.2

6"

5"

FIG.3.

FIG. 6.

FIG.7.

$3 \times 1\frac{1}{4}$

$4'' \times 4''$

$3 \times \frac{3}{4}$

2'.3"

3'.6"

2'.6"

6'. 0."

FIG.4.

FIG.5

GARDEN GATE

Full dimensions for making a strong garden gate are given in the diagrams on the next page. The design, as will be seen in the front view at Fig. 1, is one suitable for use with the wooden fencing on page 195, but it will be in keeping with any form of wooden fence or a low brick wall. If possible the gate should be made in oak, but deal may be preferred, as it is easier to work.

Owing to the strain thrown on gate posts it is advisable to set them in concrete as shown at Fig. 2; if the gate posts should form the ends of the fence, this should be attended to when erecting the fence posts. In preparing the posts as indicated at Fig. 3, the possibility of obtaining them shaped from stout material should not be overlooked.

The construction of the gate is shown in detail at Fig. 4. The three rails are tenoned into the outside uprights, the tenons may be carried right through or sawn to a length of 3 in., but in this case the mortise should be $3\frac{1}{2}$ in. deep to allow for drawing in the tenon by means of hard wood pegs as shown in the detail at Fig. 5. The method to be followed is to bore the hole in the tenon a trifle nearer the shoulder, this will allow of the shoulder being drawn upright when the peg is driven in.

It will be seen that the upright pieces or slats between the top and second rails are let in slots, but those between the second and bottom rails, can be fitted in grooves. If the lower portion of the gate is filled in with narrow tongued and grooved boards, it will help in strengthening the construction. The cross struts should be fitted after the gate has been framed up, the corners should be a tight fit and the two pieces are halved together as shown at Fig. 7.

Gates should be hung on strong hinges, although butt hinges can be used, it is advisable to use those provided with a strap or arm.

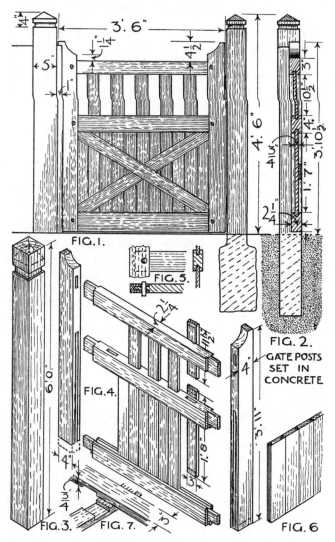

1¼"

3' 6"

1¼"

4½"

5"

1"

4' 6"

3"

10½"

4"

3.10½"

4¼"

1' 7"

2¼"

FIG. 1.

FIG. 5.

FIG. 2.
GATE POSTS
SET IN
CONCRETE

2¼"

1½"

4"

6' 0"

FIG. 4.

1' 8"

3"

3.11"

4"

¾"

FIG. 3.

FIG. 7.

3"

FIG. 6

GARDEN ARCHES

The three types of garden arches shown on the next page are typical of useful forms of construction. The arch at Fig. 1 is made from so-called rustic wood, actually it is larch or fir, with the bark left on the poles. Suitable dimensions for the arch are given at Fig. 2, and included at Fig. 3 are details of the joints. At least 4 ft. of the upright poles should be buried in the ground.

A form of arch for use with 2 in. by 2 in. wood is shown at Fig. 4. Dimensions are given at Fig. 5 and details of the joints at Fig. 6. The material should be obtained machined-planed to 2 in. by 2 in. ; this will mean that the rough timber will measure $2\frac{1}{4}$ in. by $2\frac{1}{4}$ in. It may be easy to get some $2\frac{1}{2}$ in. by $2\frac{1}{2}$ in. wood planed down, if so it should be used, as the small extra thickness will not matter. In ordering the wood do not forget the extra 3 ft. and 4 ft. to let in the ground.

The arch shown at Fig. 7 can be made from $1\frac{1}{2}$ in. by $1\frac{1}{2}$ in. wood and, when made to the dimensions given in the two elevations at Fig. 8, has a pleasing appearance. There are four uprights in each standard, these should be from 7 ft. to 8 ft. above the ground and about 4 ft. below ground. The uprights are spaced $1\frac{1}{2}$ in. apart, this can be done by separate $1\frac{1}{2}$ in. lengths nailed on, but the better way is to cut out some $4\frac{1}{2}$ in. by $4\frac{1}{2}$ in. blocks from $1\frac{1}{2}$ in. wood and notch the corners $1\frac{1}{2}$ in. each way. The standards should be fitted with a cap as shown at Fig. 9, cut from $1\frac{1}{2}$ in. wood, $7\frac{1}{2}$ in. by $7\frac{1}{2}$ in., with a chamfer under. The top of the arch can be arranged at any convenient height as it will fit between the uprights of the standard and is nailed directly to them.

The importance of protecting the lower portion of the uprights which are sunk in the ground must not be overlooked, char or coat them with pitch. With single post uprights it is advisable to set them in concrete.

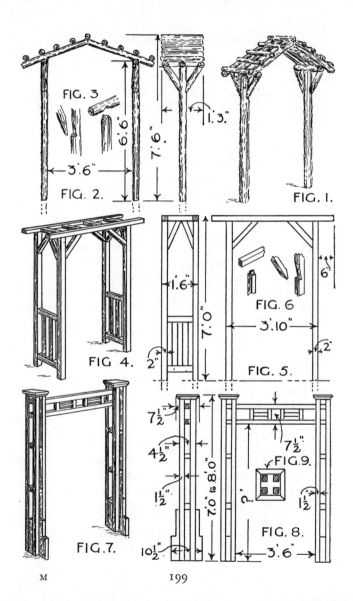

FIG. 3

6'.6"

7'.6"

3'.6"

FIG. 2.

1'.3"

FIG. I.

FIG 4.

1'.6"

7'.0"

2"

FIG. 6

3'.10"

2'

6"

2"

FIG. 5.

FIG.7.

7½"

4½"

1½"

7'.0" to 8'.0"

10½"

2'

7½"

FIG.9.

1½"

2"

FIG. 8.

3'.6"

PERGOLAS

The simple design at Fig. 1 can be made with 3 in. by 3 in. and 3 in. by 1½ in. wood. First decide on the total length and a suitable width, the latter may range from 4 ft. to 6 ft., usually the wider dimension is a more suitable one. The height is generally about 6 ft., but it should not be lower and may, with advantage, be higher. The side standards should be from 15 in. to 18 in. wide, and spaced out approximately 6 ft. apart, but the actual distance will depend on the total length.

The outside uprights of the 3 in. by 3 in. standards should be sunk into the ground at least 3 ft., this allowance being made when obtaining the material. The intermediate uprights and the cross bars are 3 in. by 1½ in; the latter may be let into grooves cut on the outside pieces and the uprights nailed on, or they may be tenoned and joined to the uprights with halving joints. The top members should be of 3 in. by 3 in. material.

The design at Fig. 2 can be made with 2 in. by 2 in. wood, the corner posts of the standards being from 12 in. to 15 in. apart.

If made in oak, the cross bars should be tenoned to the uprights, with deal they may be nailed, but as the wood is easy to work a much more satisfactory result is obtained with joints. The standards should, of course, be sunk at least 3 ft. in the ground. The wood should be treated as advised on page 198.

The design at Fig. 3 provides some interesting work in brick-laying, as described on page 174. The top rails should be of stout material, 4 in. by 4 in. or more, and the cross members spaced about 18 in. apart, from 5 in. by 3 in. material, and project at least 9 in. on each side. The cross members can be notched into the rails or skew nailed.

Another method of making the uprights is to provide suitable moulds and cast in cement.

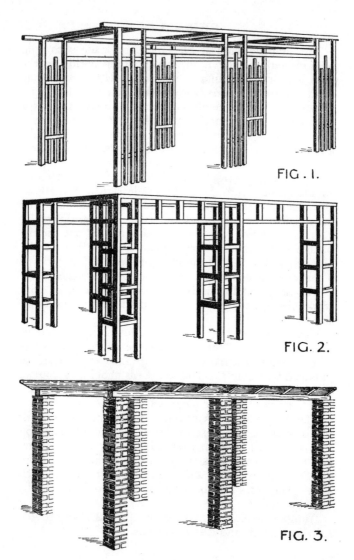

FIG. 1.

FIG. 2.

FIG. 3.

FOLDING GARDEN HAMMOCKS

The hammock stand shown at Fig. 1 is useful for a garden where it is impossible to sling an ordinary hammock between two convenient trees or posts. It has the added advantage of folding flat so that it can be stored away during the winter.

The framework, if possible, should be in hardwood, and in this case made entirely of $1\frac{1}{2}$ in. by $\frac{7}{8}$ in. material; but if clean deal is used, that is timber comparatively free from knots, it should be 2 in. by $1\frac{1}{8}$ in. The main dimensions are given in Fig. 1.

The best method of arriving at the angle of the end pieces is shown at Fig. 2, and in order to set out the correct slope, mark out the dotted lines on a table or on the floor, and support the pieces on an upright 2 ft. 6 in. high. The sloping pieces at the end are shown at Fig. 3 and are hinged together with a brass plate as at Fig. 4.

In order to prevent fraying, the sharp edges of the end pieces should be slightly rounded and smoothed with glasspaper.

Prepare the bottom members to 7 ft. long, and the four cross struts to 8 ft. 6 in., and secure to the sloping ends with bolts and nuts, similar to those used in a deck chair, although stout screws may be used. The width between the bottom lengths is 3 ft. In order to prevent them spreading, a $\frac{1}{4}$ in. diameter iron rod with ends bent at right angles should be provided and fitted into screw eyes on the inside as shown at Fig. 5.

The canopy shown in Fig. 1 is an added luxury, it is supported by a framing of $\frac{1}{4}$ in. round iron rod and light brass tubing. The rods are arranged as shown at Fig. 6 to fit into screw eyes driven in the end pieces. It will be seen at Fig. 7, that the top of the rods fit into the brass tubing, the other ends being bent to fit into the screw eyes. The canopy is made from canvas with a suitable fringed edge.

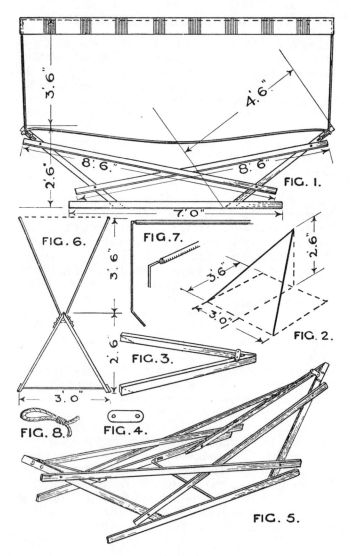

3'.6"

4'.6"

8'.6"

8'.6"

2'.6"

FIG. 1.

7'.0"

FIG. 6.

FIG. 7.

3'.6"

2'.6"

3'.6"

3'.0"

FIG. 2.

2'.6"

FIG. 3.

FIG. 8.

FIG. 4.

3'.0"

FIG. 5.

GARDEN SEAT IN OAK

To make the seat shown on the next page it is advisable to use oak on account of its durability under all weather conditions. It is, of course, possible to use deal which is much easier to work and cheaper to buy, but it will require frequent painting to preserve the wood.

The measurements of the various parts are given in the details of construction, these are so arranged and lettered that the relation of one part to the other can be followed quite easily from the diagram.

It is as well to make the two ends first. The back upright A should be sloped from the front, working from a line 1 ft. 8 in. up from the bottom to a thickness of 1 in. at the top. This will provide sufficient slope for the back of the seat. The arm at C should not be marked out until the seat rail D and the bottom rail E, as shown in the separate details, have been cut and shaped, and all fitted in position.

When both lots of framing for the ends have been made, they should be glued and pinned together with oak pins, fitted as shown at Fig. 5 on page 197. Care should be taken in trimming the oak pegs, saw off as close as possible and then pare them with a sharp chisel.

The back, comprising two 4 ft. by 4 in. by 1 in. lengths, F and G, is made up completely, together with five 13 in. by 4 in. by 1 in. slats. The end dovetails should be cut, and the upright slats H tenoned in $\frac{3}{4}$ in. deep, as shown. The seat rail at K should also be prepared with the front edge rounded as shown, and care should be taken to see that the shoulders of all the lengths at F, G and K are all exactly the same distance apart. Fit these parts in position and check the measurement of the bottom rail L which is tenoned into the side rails E. When ready glue up the parts and pin together. Finally cut the seat laths to size and either nail or screw them in position as shown.

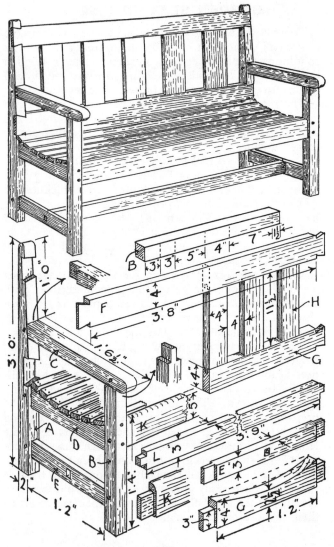

RE-STRINGING A RACKET

Although considerable skill is necessary before the art of re-stringing of a match racket can be carried out with perfect success, it is quite possible to make a satisfactory job of a practice or children's racket. The gut is supplied in 21 in. lengths for mains and in 18 in. lengths for crossings (red). Trebling gut is in 18 in. lengths. There is no need to use best quality unless a first class racket is being strung.

Begin by removing all the broken gut and then thoroughly clean the frame and holes; these are shown numbered at Fig. 1, so that the stringing, partly done at Fig. 2, can be followed without difficulty. It is as well at this stage to give the frame a coat of french polish or shellac varnish. Tie a length of gut from A to B (Fig. 2) to draw the frame to the correct width.

Start stringing as shown at Fig. 2 by threading a length of main gut through the hole at 1 to the holes at 2 at the top holes numbered 1. Cross the two lengths and thread through the same holes to bring the gut down to 2 at the bottom.

Working on one side, carry the gut up through 3 to 2 at the top, from 3 at the top carry down to 4 at the bottom and so on. The end of the last thread on each side is carried in and out of the outside loops at the bottom as shown at Fig. 2.

The crossings are strung as at Figs. 3 and 4, pegs being driven in as at P (Fig. 4) to keep the frame in shape as the work progresses. The method of threading the trebling gut is shown at Fig. 5. Care should be taken to keep the threading of the trebling gut quite even and tight. Each upright length should be kept parallel. New lengths of gut are secured at Fig. 6. The lacing hook shown at C is used for pulling the gut tight and the awl at D for forming a passage for the gut; both these tools can be home made.

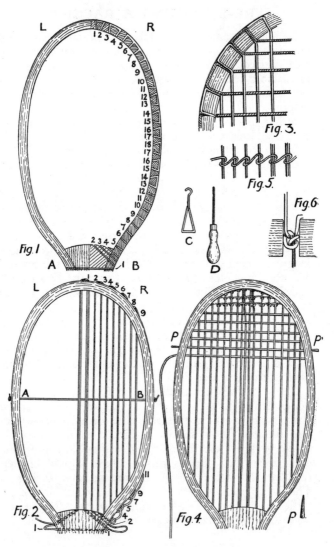

Fig. 1.

Fig. 2.

Fig. 3.

Fig. 5.

Fig. 6.

C

D

Fig. 4.

GARDEN SHELTER

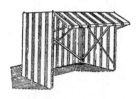

This folding shelter is a useful garden fitment for the summer. There are actually three separate parts in the main framework although they are joined together. One is the framing for the back (Fig. 1) and two sides, one being shown at Fig. 2. The top framing Fig. 3 is separate and one straight length is required for the front. Birch, machine-planed to size, should be used.

For the parts marked A and D prepare four lengths 5 ft. 10 in. by 1¼ in. by 1¼ in. All the remaining lengths are 1 in. by ⅞ in. Cut the lengths to the outside dimensions: it will be seen that the two lengths B are 5 ft. 9 in., those at E are 4 ft. 10⅜ in., at F, 10⅜ in., at H, 5 ft. 1⅜ in. Check all measurements carefully to avoid waste.

When all the lengths have been cut to size, remembering that the parts marked E, F, L and M must be duplicated, the various holes must be bored for the rivets as shown at Fig. 4; these are ⅛ in. diameter. Cut off the rivets to 2⅜ in. for the A and D uprights, and 2 in. for the remainder. Washers will be required for each rivet. The centre marking for the rivet holes is given in each case, each pair being checked. The rivets should be closed over the washers as at Fig. 5 following the method described at Figs. 1, 2 and 3 on page 39.

Two metal fitments (Fig. 6) are required for one end of the pieces M, these can be made of sheet brass, two more (Fig. 7) will be needed at the other end of the same lengths. The spikes on the top of the uprights should project 1 in. and should be fitted into holes carefully drilled. The canvas cover may be made to fit similarly to the shelter on page 211. The length of the shelter when open is 5 ft. 10 in., and the width 3 ft. 2½ in.

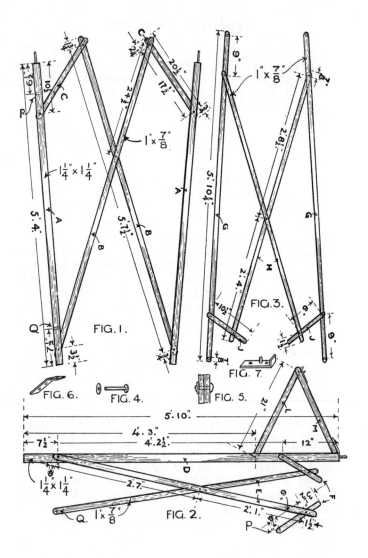

FIG. 1.

FIG. 2.

FIG. 3.

FIG. 4.

FIG. 5.

FIG. 6.

FIG. 7.

PORTABLE GARDEN TENT

The tent shown at Fig. 1 is suitable for use at the seaside as well as in the garden. With the supports made of bamboo, the tent will be light enough to carry about, and by dividing the supports in two halves and fitting sleeve joints, the tent can be packed up in a comparatively small parcel. For use in the garden birch uprights can be used.

The layout of the canvas covering is shown at Fig. 2. The material should be 2 yards wide and the measurements given allow for a 1 in. hem on three sides with a 4 in. deep pocket. The latter, shown in the separate detail at Fig. 3, is sewn up in sections and will be found useful when the tent is used for bathing purposes as the pockets can be filled with sand to steady the tent instead of using guy ropes. All sewing should be done with strong linen thread and particular attention should be given to the sewing of the pockets on the bottom edges.

To allow the canvas to be fitted on the top of the poles, the holes at the top corners should be button-holed with string as shown at Fig. 4. Narrow webbing as shown at Fig. 5 should be sewn on the sides at intervals. Six poles should be provided as shown at Fig. 6, the ends of the bamboo should be fitted with pieces of wood and bound with wire as shown at Fig. 7, care being taken that this is done at a suitable distance from the inside joint of the bamboo as at Fig. 8. Short lengths of iron rod are now driven in as indicated at Fig. 9. The top ends of the guy ropes should be fastened round metal thimbles as at Fig. 10. Tent pegs as shown at Fig. 11, made of beech or birch, will be required, but when used in the lawn more suitable alternatives are lengths of iron rod as shown at Fig. 12. Toggles made of hard wood to the sizes shown at Fig. 13 are fitted on the other ends of the guy ropes as shown at Fig. 14.

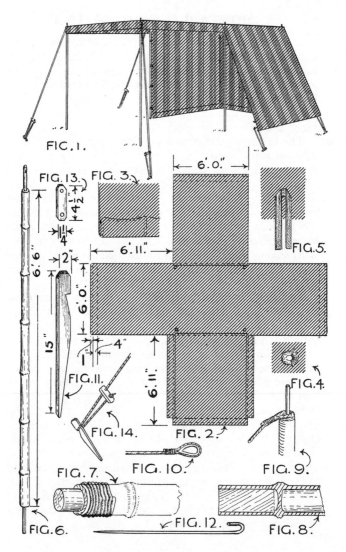

FIG. 1.

FIG. 13.

$4\frac{1}{2}$

$\frac{11}{4}$

FIG. 3.

FIG. 5.

6'.0."

6'.11."

6'.0."

2"

15

1"   4"

FIG. 11.

6'.11."

FIG. 14.

FIG. 2.

FIG. 4.

FIG. 9.

FIG. 10.

6'.6"

FIG. 7.

FIG. 6.

FIG. 12.

FIG. 8.

INDEX

INDEX

INDEX

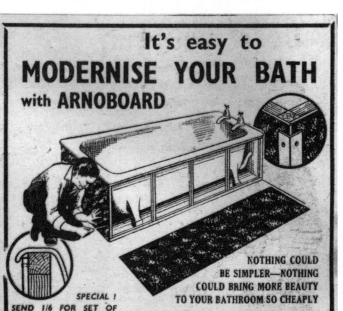

Old fashioned table — becomes Contemporary favourite

It's amazingly simple to turn old kitchen furniture into bright, labour-saving pieces, by resurfacing with WARERITE Handy Panels. The new surfaces are hard-wearing, easy-to-clean, and spilt food will not stain them. WARERITE Handy Panels are genuine WARERITE Laminated Plastic Veneers already *press-bonded* to quality plywood. Fixing is easy. All you have to do is glue wood to wood—using any ordinary cold glue.

Ask your local Ironmonger or Builders' Merchant to show you the wonderful range of WARERITE Patterns. You'll be sure to find an attractive design to match your decorative scheme.

Give a new lease of life to your
KITCHEN TABLES · DRESSERS · BEDSIDE AND COFFEE TABLES · CUPBOARDS OR CABINETS SHELVES · TRAYS

Available in five standard sizes:
24" x 18", 30" x 18", 24" x 24", 36" x 24", 48" x 24", Or any size cut to your requirement, up to 96" x 48" max.

WARERITE
REGD. TRADE MARK
Handy Panels

WARERITE LIMITED (Unit of Bakelite Limited)
WARE · HERTS. Tel: WARE 502

The quickest—safest—easiest paint remover

'RIPPING'

STRIPS ALL PAINTS, ENAMEL, CELLULOSE, EMULSION PAINT AND DISTEMPER—*says Painter Bill*

The makers of those decorator's quality paints—Brolac and Murac P.E.P.—now make available to you their special paint remover. 'Ripping' is used by professional decorators for quick, safe and easy stripping of all types of paint, enamel, cellulose, emulsion paint and distemper. It is non-caustic and non-inflammable and can therefore be used with perfect safety. Ready for use in liquid form.

MADE BY THE MAKERS OF BROLAC AND MURAC P.E.P.
and available from all stockists of those decorator's quality products.

Modernise your home!

with CELOTEX
REGD TRADE MARK

FIVE-STAR Door Panels

6'6 Each

This is the answer to the problem of modernising out-of-date recess-panelled doors. The pre-cut Celotex Five-Star Door Panel eliminates the troublesome job of removing the door. In a matter of minutes the door panel can be fixed, ready for painting, graining, papering or other decorative finishes.

This is the easiest way ever of transforming your doors and obtaining a bright, contemporary effect at a *really low cost*!

The Celotex Five-Star Door Panels are made from tough, grainless, high density hardboard, specially heat-treated for extra strength and resistance to wear. Send today for full details and the name of your local stockist.

CELOTEX LIMITED

NORTH CIRCULAR ROAD, STONEBRIDGE PARK, LONDON,
N.W.10. TEL : ELGAR 5717 (10 LINES).

Post this today

CELOTEX LIMITED, NORTH CIRCULAR ROAD, STONEBRIDGE
PARK, LONDON. N.W.10.

Please send me, without obligation, full details of Celotex Five-Star Door Panels.

NAME ....

ADDRESS ....

Women
give it no rest!

DAY in and day out, it is hard at work.

You take its efficiency for granted—it is your vacuum cleaner.

Ask your wife about it—she uses it every day for cleaning carpets, furniture, stairs, curtains easily and without any fuss.

But are you sure your cleaner is really safe and really efficient ? Compare it with the latest Vactric. If you haven't bought a cleaner yet, see a Vactric first.

Fill in this coupon and we'll let you and your wife know all about the latest Vactric models which you can still buy on easy terms. We make a generous allowance on your old cleaner.

(*Note to wives : If he needs any extra persuasion, tell him about the optional spray-gun attachment !*)

MAKE LIFE EASY WITH
VACTRIC

BANKRUPT STOCK

HAVING BOUGHT STOCKS OF SEVERAL FIRMS IN LIQUIDATION WE ARE NOW OFFERING SAME AT A HANDOUT. ORDER NOW AND EARN YOUR CHRISTMAS EXPENSES. CALLERS WELCOME.

GOLLIWOGS. The old Favourite Black-face Gollys over 22" tall with fuzzy hair, bright coloured Jackets, fancy striped Trousers, white shirt and contrast bow. Worth 21/-. **Note our Price Each 8/9.**

GIANT TEDDY BEARS. What a cuddle. This smashing Bear is 34in. tall in either Golden Brown, Beauty Pink or Sky Blue Rich Silky Fur Plush. Will stand up or sit down. Finished with growler voice and wide satin bow at neck. Worth 63/- each retail. **Each 32/6.**

FANCY BUTTONS for Coats or Frocks. High Class West End stock which will beautify any garment. Made to sell originally from 3/11 to 9/11 dozen retail. Each gross is made up of 4 different designs and colours, 36 buttons to a design. Why not try a carton of 444 buttons in 12 different styles for 20/-. Note our price **6/6** per gross buttons.

MEN'S BRACES in solid leather nut brown tan, finished with stout elastic insert at back for ease and comfort. Ex-Officers stock which cost the Government 9/3 pair originally. **12/9 per dozen pairs.**

TOY PANDAS. Giant size in the popular sit up style. 20in. high overall. In rich Luxurious Black and White Fur Fabric finished with Contrasting Leather Paws, Googly Eyes, Squeaker Voice and Satin Bow at neck. Will sell easily for 25/-. **Note our price, 14/6 Each.**

FANCY RIBBONS in a lovely assortment of Satins, Cordeds, Moires, Tartans, Taffetas, Checks and Fancies in Nylon and Bright Rayon from ¼" right up to 6" wide. In White, Pink, Peach, Sky, Nil, Black, Sax, Royal Navy, Brown, Silver and Gold. All in 6 yard lengths. Perfect goods worth up to 2/11 yard retail. **Per Parcel of 50 yds. Asstd. 10/-.**

LACE EDGINGS in Nylon and Bright Rayon. Lovely designs in White, Pink, Sky, Peach, Ecru, Lemon, Nil, Red, etc., for trimming underwear, frocks, etc. From ⅛" up to 1" wide. Pick your own colours. Worth 9d. yard. **Per Gross Yards 12/6**

HANDY WIRE, single strand P.V.C. covered, extra strong, will withstand strain of 560 lbs. Suitable for Phone Cable, Garden Work, Tying, Baling, Toy Makers, etc., Full 3,000ft. Drums, ex-Govt. stock which cost originally 55/-. Our Price PER DRUM (3,000ft.) £2/9.

TOY BALLOONS. Always a fast seller. The famous Fantasia. Dunlop and other well-known brands. All triple dipped pure Latex warranted 100 per cent. perfect, no duds. Packed in Flashy Counter cases in asstd. colours or bright jazz mixtures. Giant size, 100cm. **27/- gross.** Large size, 70cm. round **17/- gross.**

MAMA DOLLS. Every girl will go for this beauty. Large 20in. doll, most realistic with sleeping eyes, mama voice, moving arms and legs. Permanently waved hair and head turns from side to side. Blonde or Brunette. Dressed in smart silky Taffeta frock with Hat to match, finished large bow. Real plastic Ankle strap shoes and White Bobby Sox. Worth 39/11 in any high class shop. **Note Our Price each, 23/6.**

BRIDE DOLLS. The Princess Grace full 22" Length Bride Doll dressed in a lovely Beauty Rayon White Wedding Gown with Gold Trimmed Head-dress and fancy trimmed Bridal Veil, White socks and Plastic Shoes. Finished with Mama voice and Sleeping eyes. Blonde or Brunette with permanently waved hair. Worth 63/-. **Each 27/6**

ZIP JACKETS for Boys or Girls. Full Hip length with open end Zip Front. Two pockets. Elastic Gathered Waist and windproof Cuffs. In Satinised Gaberdine 100% Waterproof with attractive lining to tone. In Wine, Blue or Green. Worth Double. 24" length **22/6 each.** 18", 20" and 22" Length. **19/9 Each.**

SEND P.O. AND ORDER TODAY FOR DELIVERY BY RETURN AND START MAKING SOME DECENT PROFIT FOR A CHANGE. ORDERS OVER £2 SENT POST FREE.

PHILIP WINNER & CO.
65, FARRINGDON ROAD, HOLBORN, LONDON, E.C.1

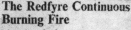

You can have tile-bright walls...

for less than 1/- a square foot with

CONGOWALL

Wonderful stuff, Congowall! For less than a shilling a square foot you can have kitchen or bathroom walls that look like tile, feel like tile, and clean like tile. And you can very easily put up Congowall yourself, following the simple directions supplied. It's a simple weekend job that will give you lasting pride and satisfaction.

Congowall's finish resists dirt and wet just like tile. Like tile it lasts and lasts. A rub over with a damp cloth is all that's needed to clean it. You can choose from a number of charming colours.

Draw chalk line at a height of 4′ 6″—or less if you like, in which case cut a strip off the bottom of the roll of Congowall.

Spread special Congowall adhesive on one convenient length at a time.

Apply Congowall cut to length. Rub with a damp cloth or roller.

Ask your household stores or builder's merchant to show you samples and pattern book. In case of difficulty send p.c. to British Congoleum Ltd., Dept. CW/37, 131 Aldersgate Street, London, E.C.1.

A BRITISH CONGOLEUM PRODUCT

Published about the 7th of each month by GEORGE NEWNES LIMITED, Tower House, Southampton Street, Strand, London, W.C.2, and Printed in England by W. Speaight & Sons, Exmoor Street, London, W.10. Sole Agents for South Africa—Central News Agency, Ltd. Subscription Rate (including postage): For one year, Inland 20s., Abroad 18s. (Canada 16/6). Registered at the G.P.O. for transmission by Canadian Magazine Post.

"Practical Householder" Advice Bureau COUPON. This coupon is available until November 7th, 1956, and must be attached to all letters containing queries. A stamped, addressed envelope must also be enclosed.
Practical Householder   November, 1956.

Only **ASBESTOLUX**

Does so many jobs so well

... safe, good-looking wall-mounting for an electric panel fire.

... neat hood over a cooker and air vent... and an Asbestolux ceiling prevents condensation.

... box in an old-fashioned bath and line the ceiling, you can then paint, paper or tile it.

AND lots of other jobs too!

Only **ASBESTOLUX**

Is so easy to work

Saw it *Drill it* *Nail it* *Paint it*

Only **ASBESTOLUX**

Has so many advantages

Fire will not hurt it

Time will not harm it

Water will not damage it

Vermin will not touch it

Yes—it's true! Asbestolux will do all these things and more! Strong, light, rigid, durable, Asbestolux is the fire-safe board that saves endless time and labour. You can cut, shape, drill, punch, nail, screw, file and finish it at record speeds; it won't twist, bend or warp; can't swell or move when wet. *And you can give it a fine finish*—paint it, wall-paper it, tile it! *Only* ASBESTOLUX does all this for you—see your local supplier and ask for free illustrated booklet, or write to us for details.

ASBESTOLUX

the fire-safe board for the handyman in a hurry

 CAPE BUILDING PRODUCTS LIMITED
COWLEY BRIDGE WORKS · UXBRIDGE · MIDDLESEX
A subsidiary of The Cape Asbestos Company Ltd.
Also at:—MANCHESTER · BIRMINGHAM · GLASGOW · NEWCASTLE

AX13

NOTES

_____

_____

_____

_____

_____

_____

_____

_____

_____

_____

_____

_____

_____

_____

NOTES

NOTES